I0606436

HARRY CLARK

HARRY

Staying Faithful

CLARK.

spck

First published in Great Britain in 2025

SPCK
SPCK Group
Studio 101
The Record Hall
16–16A Baldwin's Gardens
London EC1N 7RJ
spckpublishing.co.uk

Photographs courtesy of the author unless otherwise stated.

EU GPSR Authorised Representative
LOGOS EUROPE, 9 rue Nicolas Poussin, 17000, La Rochelle, France
Email: Contact@logoseurope.eu

British Library Cataloguing-in-Publication Data
A catalogue record for this book is available from the British Library

ISBN 978-0-281-09222-2
eBook ISBN 978-0-281-09221-5

1 3 5 7 9 10 8 6 4 2

Typeset by Westchester Publishing Services
First printed in Great Britain by Clays Ltd

eBook by Westchester Publishing Services

Produced on paper from sustainable sources

I promise that everything in this book is the truth.
And you can believe me this time.

Contents

List of plates

INTRODUCTION

THE NIGHT OF *The Traitors* final, there is a huge storm. Four weeks ago, there had been twenty-two of us. Now, there are only four. I remember everything I've been through—not just on the show but in my life in general—and I realise how lucky I am to be here.

I also can't believe I've gotten this far. My friends and family think I'm the worst liar in the world. My dad says my poker face is rubbish, and I've never yet been able to get a fib past my mum. When I told them I was going to do this, neither of them knew what to say, apart from 'but you can never keep a straight face!'. They know me too well. I haven't spoken to them now for almost a month, which feels weird, because I love my family and I would do anything for them. That's why I'm here. Having grown up in a council house in Slough, I know that this money—almost £100k—is more than any of us is likely to see in our lifetime. How amazing would it be to tell them I'd won? Not that they'd care. My dad only wants me to come home safe, and if I called my mum after four weeks, she'd probably just say it's nice to hear my voice. But that's how much they love me, and I want to give something back to them. I couldn't care less about the cameras or the fame, or the fact that this is one of the biggest shows on the telly. I'm here because I want to better the lives of my family. And I couldn't have put myself in a better position than I am now to win that money.

On the first day we arrived at the castle, it was filled with people, everyone moving around, literally buzzing with excitement. I can remember at the time thinking a million things: What are the other contestants going to be like? How am I going to cope with an accusation? What's my tactic in the game as a whole? Am I a Faithful or do I get to be a Traitor? My head was so full of noise, I could barely tell what I was thinking. But tonight, that noise has gone. I am focused. I know there's no point in having a game plan because anything can happen. Everything that's happened in the last four weeks has been chaos. But I know that if I can keep my nerve, if I can respond in the right way to my fellow finalists, if I can convince everyone that I'm faithful (just as I have for weeks), if I can hold it together, and if I can be Harry the Traitor for just one more hour, then I can win.

My mind goes quiet, and I can hear the silence in the room. Suddenly, I know what I want to do . . . I want to sing 'Fly Me to the Moon' by Frank Sinatra. One of his best and my karaoke classic. And I start singing.

Fly me to the moon, Frank.

My mum always called me the 'wonky pancake'. I've got a lot of brothers and sisters—there are five of us—and she said that whenever you make a bunch of pancakes, one of them is always going to be a bit different. Well, I guess that's me. Always ready to do the most random stuff, take a risk, just go for it. I've never been one to be put in a box, and if someone says I can't do something, that makes me want to do it even more. I see a challenge and run towards it.

When I was eight or nine years old, I asked my mum if we could go to Disneyland (Florida) on a Wednesday after school. I kept moaning on and on about it, and it drove her nuts. What I didn't understand then was the reality of raising five kids. I had no idea of the sacrifices my parents had already made for the family and, believe me, they did so much. My dad has never stopped working so he could support us, taking whatever job he needed to and even being away sometimes. All the while, my mum was raising us kids brilliantly—even when she was studying for a nursing degree. That alone showed me how you can do anything you set your mind to, and just as my parents demonstrated that to me, I want to prove it back to them.

Maybe this is a little bit dark for so early on in the book, but the other day I was walking through a graveyard near where I live, looking at headstones and thinking a lot about my life. It seems to me that a graveyard is a place of unanswered dreams. How much beautiful music wasn't released by people who are now in the ground? How many films and TV shows and radio series and podcasts and other types of art weren't created? How many businesses weren't started or brilliant ideas explored? Sometimes, we're just too afraid to do the scary thing or to take a leap and see where it lands us.

As I stood in the graveyard, I thought: I never want to be that person lying there not having given something a go. In fact, I want to be in the ground with a sort of smile, knowing that I gave everything my best. Because the parts of our lives we give everything to are the parts that grow us, that fill us up and that make us believe, not just in ourselves, but in the world.

Some people will look at my life now and say, of course, I feel able to do all this stuff, now that I have a bit of money in the bank (I've still not worked out how to spend most of my winnings) and some new Instagram followers. But honestly, that isn't what gives me confidence to go out and feel like I can do anything every day. Money has never meant much to me, and I only see fame as a tool for helping to spread positive vibes around the world. What gives me strength in my life are the relationships I've built and continue to maintain: with my family, with my friends and with my girlfriend, Anna. I also get a lot of energy from the parts of my life that bring me so much joy: boxing, football, running, music, gaming, Chelsea FC and making people around me laugh (I'm an entertainer). And so, these are the things that I devote myself to fully. I go to the gym every morning because I know it makes me the best person for those around me for the rest of the day. I joined the Army to learn a trade I could use to support the family I have now and any family I might have in the future. And I went on *The Traitors*—four solid weeks away from everyone I love and no idea of what was going to happen—to win it. I know that the energy I'm putting in is going to come back to me and that, ultimately, everything will work out in the end (and yes, I'm still talking about death, sorry).

When I tell people about this attitude, this confidence in the future, this belief in things getting better, I call it manifestation, and that resonates with almost anyone I'm speaking to. It's also what I feel about religion. Religion has always seemed like these ideas that are written in stone or that are studied and examined by great minds and then passed down to us. But one thing I've definitely learnt from my dad is that it doesn't have to be that deep. I think it's much more simple and much more personal than that.

In my life, my faith has become stronger and weaker at different times. I'm going to tell you the whole story in this book and reveal that there were occasions when I really questioned my faith and almost entirely lost the part of myself that believed. In some dark moments, I almost gave up on life. In the Army, especially, you see how beautiful life is and how wonderful it can be, but you also see that it can be cruel and short.

My favourite way to understand my faith is to imagine myself as a vase, like the ones you put flowers in. If you threw the vase off the table, it would smash into a hundred different shards. Everyone in my life who I'm closest to—my mum, my dad, Anna, my brothers, my sisters, my mates—they all love me and I love them, but they all have a different piece of the vase. They don't fully know who I am because they only have a piece, and each piece is different. I don't think you can be the same for every person you meet, because each one you meet is different. And when the vase shatters, it can be hard to put it back together. But to me, faith is believing that God not only knows what the vase looks like when it's whole, but that he can also start helping me put the pieces back together when they're on the floor. This gives me a sense of calmness and security in my life. I trust that whatever I'm doing, God can see me, knows I'm trying my best, and has a plan for me. The way I look at it is that you never know what's going to happen tomorrow or in your life in general, so there's no use worrying about it. Just do your best, stay present to the great things you have around you, and you'll become thankful for your life, and thankfulness is really the thing that makes it great. Doing all this is how I started to put my own life back together.

So, while people still ask me all the time if I go to church on Sunday, I actually think that church isn't a place we go to once a week, but rather, it's within us, helping us along and guiding us every day. I believe I can be just as close to God sitting on the end of my bed having a little pray as I can when I'm in church. I believe church is in how we look at the world, how we move in it and how we deal with whatever comes to us. My faith gives me the confidence to try something new, to do the thing that scares me, and to face the new challenge.

For me right now, this book is that challenge. Going through school, I was rubbish at English. I could only talk in my English class when I had a story to tell (I am quite good at that). Also, I've always been dyslexic, and that was a real problem, not just in English. So, producing an autobiography is no small thing for me. I'm excited to show it to my whole family and one day to my kids and grandkids and tell them that I never, in my entire life, imagined writing a book.

But I'm not just doing this because I want to prove something to myself. I'm doing it because I've had a crazy life, and even in my twenty-four years on this earth, I feel like I've learnt a lot. I'm grateful to be in a position to share those lessons. I want to encourage people through their own dark times by explaining what got me through, and then talk about what brings me happiness in life today, just in case it's of use to anyone else out there. For me, a big part of religion is about passing on good ideas and supporting people, so if I can help one person, then my job here is done. And if they help someone else, then we have a great karma chain that can just continue on.

I hope that in reading this book, you find your own faith, your own sense of purpose and the things that get you through and bring you joy. Because that's what it's all about . . . joy. I love being able to bring that to anyone, and it's what I love to hear from people now about *The Traitors*: how it gave them an escape, how it brought them together and how happy it made them. (See, I told you I was an entertainer.)

So, I hope you find joy in this book. I have faith in you.

1
MUM

I WANT TO START by writing about my mum. Both of my parents are really strong, so I guess I'd call my mum the strongest woman ever. And though that may sound like an exaggeration, I'm not sure it quite does her justice. She is Superwoman to me.

My dad was the breadwinner, the one who would make sure we were always looked after financially (among other things—Dad, skip to your chapter!). But while he was away at work, my mum was there for us all of the time. She raised us with a huge amount of care and attention, giving each of us everything we needed, which is amazing when she had so many kids. We all joke about who the favourite is—one week I'll say it's me, the next week we'll say it's my little brother, the next it's my little sister—but, in fact, there's never a favourite. You feel that with my mum and dad, but my mum especially, that she never needed favourites because she has so much love to give. Ultimately, she just wants her children to be happy, and this means letting them be individuals. She helps us however she can, whether that's by creating a safe home to come back to, supporting us in our life decisions, or simply believing that we can do whatever we put our mind to, no matter how difficult.

Raising five kids is no easy thing, and I think there's an expectation with a big family that the children are going to be scruffy or naughty. I'm sure other mums in the playground would love to gossip about that, which is why my mum always made sure we were clean, didn't make trouble and were dressed in ironed clothes. She still says today that if you ever see me out and about wearing a shirt with a crease in it, you can bet I wasn't at home that morning.

She'd also make sure that all the food we ate was cooked from scratch because she knows that if children aren't fed properly, it affects their brain development. Everything was as healthy as it could be, though I didn't make that easy, as I'm a really picky eater and even now, I'd be happy just eating chicken nuggets. And so, my mum would make me chicken nuggets from scratch to make sure I wasn't eating only processed food. Can you imagine . . . home-made chicken nuggets?! They are amazing, and I still love them to this day.

One of the main ways my mum has shown us that we can do anything we set our minds to is by example. I was still at primary school when she decided she wanted to become a nurse—and then she just got on with making it happen.

The first challenge was that she needed her GCSE certificates, and Granny didn't have them. So, while my youngest sister Matilda was really little (genuinely still a baby), Mum did her Maths and English GCSEs. Then, when Matilda went to nursery, Mum completed an access to higher education course. Only after that was done could she start on her nursing degree, which was a full-time three-year course at a uni in London.

Mum used to get us up in the morning, make breakfast, get us ready (all wearing nice, clean, ironed clothes and with our hair done properly), take us to school, get on a train to London, have a full day at uni, come back to take us to any after-school activities, help us with our homework, make dinner (from scratch) and then put us to bed. Most evenings, she would go back to studying, working on her dissertation or revising for exams. I still remember so many times in the run-up to an exam when Mum and Dad would sit on the sofa together, he reading questions to her off cue-cards, and she trying to answer, with us all egging her on. My dad had no idea what he was asking (it was all very technical), but he was glad to help as he could and would read her assignments before she handed them in. He even proofread her dissertation.

During these years (and actually, even now, as she still does so much for us), I'm not sure when my mum slept. She must have struggled with tiredness at times. As a kid, you don't really take notice of what your parents do during the day, but now I'm twenty-four and an adult, I feel so impressed. I think most people on Mum's degree course were just out of school, with no responsibilities, and they were struggling with how much work there was to be done. And Mum had five kids to look after as well!

The truth is, my mum never felt that smart academically. She said she did OK in school (her favourite subjects were child development and home economics, which is where she got all her knowledge of nutrition), but like me, she's a very hands-on learner, so the lectures and reading and studying were tough. I think there were times when she wasn't sure if she'd pass her course. But she did, and now, after working through some hard years in the pandemic, she's a Senior Sister in Accident & Emergency (A&E). She's just started running her own high-dependency unit, and has forty-six staff under her. As she loves working with people, and because life is way more practical than studying, she's great at what she does and has become an expert in it. It's amazing the stuff she comes out with, like how the arteries link up, where they all lead, what signs there could be for certain diseases or what infections someone might have. I know (because we're very similar) that she would have struggled massively to learn this out of books, but obviously, she pushed through that part, and now she's so good, she's climbing the ranks.

I feel like Mum had all the odds stacked against her, and she still came out on top. I'm not sure there are a lot of people who could achieve what she has, but she taught us kids that it doesn't matter who you are, where you're from or what you have going on—whatever you set your mind to, you can do. I think I'm willing to try difficult things today because she proved to me that all it takes is willpower and hard work. I'm incredibly grateful to her for that, and really proud of her too.

In order to fit everything in, my mum would run a tight ship. She obviously made sacrifices herself, but she also kept us in line. Quick showers, strict bedtimes, and being home when dinner was ready. No messing around. Mum loves to tell stories about how she used to send me to bed, but would then have to come back in to check I was actually asleep. My light would be off when she looked under the door, but she knew it was worth double-checking that I didn't have my PSP on or something. One time, though, she didn't have to come in to check: she could hear loud music coming from the room. I was sitting under my duvet, practising my recorder, thinking that no one could hear a thing. Clearly, I've not always been so devious.

It was because of my mum's incredible love for us and her desire for us to be the best people we could be that she knew she had to discipline us. If I had to describe Mum's parenting style, I would say 'loving and strict'. Sometimes, if we were being really naughty, Mum would threaten to call Dad to tell him what we'd done, or try and get us to stop whatever we were doing, but this was funny because I was always more scared of my mum than my dad.

We all knew when Mum was angry because she'd start to show her teeth, almost like a vampire. We called it 'The Teeth', and when you saw that, you knew it was time to run. I feel sorry for her because I think she had to be the sort of head teacher of the family. If she hadn't, though, I probably would have gone off the rails, so she didn't have much choice. And she knew how to discipline me—all she had to do was take away my beloved PSP or ground me so that I couldn't go outside and play footie with my mates, and I'd be cut up. Whether I learnt my lesson or not is a different question.

Thinking about it now, I probably wasn't the easiest child to bring up. I wasn't a bad kid, and I wasn't trouble—I didn't bully people or beat up other kids for no reason. And I wouldn't be horrible to my mum or dad, or swear, or anything like that. (I still try not to swear around my mum, as she really doesn't like it.) I was more cheeky trouble. I admit, I am a little mischievous, someone who likes to push the boundaries a bit. I knew a level of respect and stuck to that, but I would also think about what I could get away with.

The best illustration of this is probably from one year when we were all on holiday. My parents tell me that when my dad worked for Lloyds Bank, he cashed in his shares and spent the money on a caravan. We used it as much as possible; having that caravan meant that no matter what was happening in the family, we'd always have a place to go on holiday. I know my mum was really happy about this because, every now and again, because of work, she'd have to miss seeing one of us play football or performing in a show (not that any of us minded); holidays gave us a chance to fully spend time together as a family.

Mind you, even if we were on holiday, we weren't allowed to miss church. Mum took us every Sunday, and she would always make sure we were up at 8 A.M. and dressed in our nice church clothes. And despite me trying to get out of it, using every excuse I could. I'd say I'd been out the night before and felt terrible, or I'd been playing in a football match and could barely walk, but it never worked. I thought being on holiday would mean we'd escape, but Mum wasn't having any of it. Imagine being a kid on summer holidays, off school and ready to have loads of fun, and you still have to get up early and go to church. It felt like a chore. And we always had smart outfits with us, just in case we needed to dress up to go out for dinner as a family or something like that.

Anyway, there was one time we went to church and we were the only family there. Everyone was so excited to see us that we got invited to a tea party afterwards. So, there we are—me, my brother Alfred and my sisters Delilah and Matilda, having just been in the grace of God for a whole hour—now in the company of a few old people. Being me, I was a little bit bored, so I bet my brother and sisters that I could eat all the sugar cubes on the big table without anyone seeing. I thought they'd find it funny. As the entertainer in the family, I loved (and still love) making them laugh. At some point during the tea party, someone realises there's no sugar left (because I've smashed every cube in sight), and it doesn't take long to work out who the culprit is, as I'm absolutely bouncing off the walls. My mum got us all out of there and home as soon as possible and gave me a serious telling-off. I can't remember the punishment or the sugar crash now, but I can't imagine either was great.

Another thing that happened regularly was my mum being phoned by my school because I'd done something or other. (At one point in Year Two, aged six, they caught me climbing out of the place because I wanted to go home!) I'll speak more about school in a later chapter, but for now, let's say that for most of the time, I just couldn't hack it. I found it boring and I struggled to learn much. I think, like Mum, I'm a physical learner and I have a hard time with anything that's not practical, or that I can't do with my hands. We are not book people. Ironic for someone writing a book, I know.

All the same, when I was at school, I really wanted to make Mum proud. You know how you get stickers for good behaviour or for doing good things? Well, I wouldn't get loads of those, so sometimes, I would pick up any that had fallen on the floor, then go home to my mum and show her all my stickers, which was maybe a little cheeky.

I think I always had good intentions, though. Mum says that one time, when I was five, I complained I was hungry and someone gave me a banana. Being really fussy about food, I hated bananas (I actually get that from my mum), and so I couldn't eat them. Instead of telling them that, though, I went into the loo and tried to flush the banana down the toilet. Unfortunately, it flooded the whole block, and my mum had to be phoned to pick me up from school yet again. Clearly always trouble, even when I don't mean to be.

On top of everything else, my mum gave us faith. Mum is the religious icon of our family, our angel, and she would always bring back holy water from church to our front door. Religion is now a big part of my life, and I get a lot of comfort and meaning from it. If it wasn't for my mum, my faith wouldn't be anywhere near as strong, and I can't thank her enough for that.

Like I said, she was the one who got us up and out to church every single week. My dad went to a Catholic school that was run by sisters. The headteacher had been there since his mum's (my nana's day), so it was a proper old-fashioned religious school. Despite this, Dad's never been into religion as such. He took Holy Communion and will always go to church if my mum asks him, but I think his faith is in prayer and knowing that whenever he's going through a tough time, he can speak to God about it.

My mum, however, will make time to go to church if she feels like she's missed a visit or needs to work something out. She was brought up Catholic and went to Catholic schools, too, but I think her upbringing was a lot stricter. She's told me that her grandfather would do Bible readings every morning and night.

Despite making us go every Sunday, she's not very dogmatic about the church, though, and allows everyone to have their own relationship with it. One of the few TV programmes my mum watched before *The Traitors* was *Eastenders,* and she says people think she's like Dot Cotton, but (unlike Dot) she doesn't push people to share her faith. As far as she's concerned, once us kids have done our Holy Communion, we've taken on faith for ourselves and can then move on however we want to.

Faith is very personal to her, and I know she still goes to church so much because she just likes going. I think it brings her a sense of calmness and comfort. And I know from speaking to her for this book that it has gotten her through some tough times and helped her find purpose in her life. When my sister Delilah got really sick and had to have heart surgery at Great Ormond Street, she prayed a lot and says now that her faith (as well as her family) was what really got her through. She always tells us that if you're ever struggling, just devote a month of your life to fully opening your heart and praying for things to get better, and it will start happening. So, I guess that's where I get my belief in manifestation through religion from.

To my mum, faith is simply believing in something you can't see and believing that God always has a plan for us. And I think that offers her a lot of peace and hope.

One of the best things about the process of doing this book has been having the excuse to ask my mum and dad loads of questions and get to know them better as people, rather than just as parents, and to hear about their lives, their relationships, their motivations and their faith.

I was thinking about some of the great times my mum and I have had together, and wondering which she would say were her favourite memories. And she did mention two that I thought would be up there: going to my Passing Out parade at Harrogate, which the whole family came to see, and hearing from me after *The Traitors*. (As I mentioned in the Introduction, she genuinely didn't care if I'd won or not.) But what surprised me was that she also chose a time when we went out for lunch on her birthday a few years ago. We only went to Bill's in Windsor and then for a walk around town, so someone looking from the outside might not believe it was anything huge. But in a big family, having a chance for just two of you to sit and talk is rare. I love getting to know my mum more as an adult and, while she's done everything for me as a kid and will always be my mum (and I'll let her keep doing my ironing, as I'm terrible at it), I'm happy that our relationship is evolving, and I'm discovering more about her as a person. It was during that lunch in Windsor that I first told her about Anna, this girl I'd met and was falling in love with, so it was a really special day.

I think I already knew that my mum's greatest joy in her life is her family. She just wants us to be happy and has done everything she can throughout our lives to make that happen. When we have a family barbecue, my mum will be there, sitting in the corner, smiling and taking photos, like a proper tourist. She wants to capture the moment, and it doesn't matter to her at all that she takes the worst photos ever!

2
DAD

THROUGHOUT MY LIFE, I've learnt a huge amount from my dad, and my family often remarks that we're incredibly similar. For example, everyone can be sitting in our living room when my dad comes in and tells a little story about what happened when he and I were out together—who we met or a small incident that took place. Five minutes later, I'll come in and tell exactly the same story. We both enjoy sharing the fun things from our day, making the people we love laugh and giving them a good time.

The entertainer in me comes from Dad. I've always thought of myself as the class clown, and that's the role he's always played himself. He'll sit in his chair and say he doesn't want to go down to the pub. 'Oh no boys, can't be bothered, blah blah blah.' As soon as he walks through the pub door, though, he knows every single person in there. You genuinely can't get a word in edgeways, because he's just met sixteen of his mates from school or something like that, and they're all chatting and drinking, having a time of it. And then, after moaning earlier that he didn't want to go to the pub in the first place, you can't get him to leave.

He's so popular because he's the funniest guy you'll ever meet. Tells great stories, some good (and some questionable) jokes, and loves to make people feel better. It can actually kind of get him into trouble with my mum. She'll never let him forget the day he left me and my older brother in a pushchair outside a pub while he 'popped in to say hi to some people'; he couldn't get into the pub with kids, so it seemed easier to park them outside. I'm not sure if he had one or two drinks, but either way, Mum wasn't happy!

It appears that before he had a family, my dad was a proper lad, going away all the time and really living it up with his mates. So, he knows how to have fun himself, and it feels really cool to have a dad who sees me as one of his best mates too.

I think it's important that your parents show you how to enjoy yourself, and my dad is definitely a role model for anyone happy to believe that life can be fun and that you can have a brilliant time. However, there's a lot more to him than that. As I said in the last chapter, I've become much more aware that parents are people too. I've found myself saying to friends who feel their childhood wasn't brilliant, try to remember that your parents had to do lots of things they'd never tried before for the first time. They're likely to have moved from having a single, carefree life to suddenly having to keep a human being alive. Or having to get up for work because they know they need to put food on the table and can't just make do with casual jobs that will allow them to have a few drinks and a kebab on the way home.

Despite the story about my dad leaving us outside a pub (sorry for sharing that, Dad), I think he did calm down a lot on the big holidays and the lads' stuff when he got together with Mum. She'd already had George, my older brother, when they met, so he became a dad straight away, and as far as he's concerned, George is his own son, no questions asked.

Which brings me onto the other role my dad plays—the provider and protector. We have fun, yeah, but he's taught me that, as a man, you need to be strong and really care for your family. And he's done everything he can to look out for my sisters, my brothers and me, always working hard and taking on whatever job he needs to, going out early and coming back late—all so he can provide for us kids.

He was in the finance industry for a while as a salesman (that's probably where I get my chat from), before deciding he was bringing too much work home when he really wanted to spend time with the young family he had, so he joined his dad and did bricklaying for fifteen years. Then, for a while, he was a baggage handler with British Airways (BA), and only left recently because his knee popped. Currently, he's helping me keep my head screwed on, which is exactly what I need right now. Basically, everything for us.

I don't even have kids yet, but I'm already thinking about giving them the best go at life. Everything I do now, every single day, is for my kids to have a better life in the future. I can hear you asking, What does that mean, the best go at life? Does it just mean money? Well, I'll tell you (and this is also something I've learnt from my dad), it's not only about that. Money is nice, obviously, and it helps you get material things like holidays in beautiful places, where you can create memories, or be able to go out for meals in restaurants every now and again, for birthdays or special celebrations. But, what I'm really thinking about is giving your kids the opportunity to be their best self through the way they treat people, love people and grow the love they have around them. I feel like my dad gave me the opportunity to be my best self in so many ways, and I want to do the same thing when I'm a dad too.

So now, when I'm going down to the gym and trying to keep fit, it's because I want to play footie with my kids in the park and share my love of sports with them. I love all sports—they bring a huge amount of joy into my life—and I'll literally play any game I can. When I work late and put energy into making money, it's because I know that I'm building towards a career that can provide for them. I don't want my kids to be spoiled, but I'd like to make sure I can buy them a new pair of football boots every year. If they want to go to uni, then great, I'll hopefully be able to support them. If they want to get married, I'd like to be able to help pay for the wedding. If they want their own kids, I'd love to be able to buy my grandchildren presents and take them on days out. As for family holidays, I'm learning French right now, as I think being able to speak to people in their native language is really smart, and I want to show that to my kids.

And, finally, knowing as I do, through my family and friends, what it's like to have a great group of people to rely on (and help when those guys need it), I want that for my kids, too.

I guess it's a bit of a contradiction, feeling it's important to live in the present moment yet thinking so much about the future, but that comes from being blessed by having the path of being a great parent laid out for me.

My family's quite traditional, in the sense that we're a really strong unit and we spend loads of time together, but I love it. I feel like nothing will break us, and that gives me a lot of purpose. I feel I've been born to work, to survive, to raise a family and then to die, having spent time with people I love. To me, that is a happy life. If that's my only purpose for being here, then why not? I can't wait to give my own little kids everything and will love them more than life itself, and that's exactly what my dad has given us.

This has probably affected my understanding of faith, too. My mum believes in our family, and it inspires what she does . . . that's my dad too. He's always said that faith means to believe in something, even when you can't always see it. The idea of family isn't something you can touch, and when my dad's at work during the day, or even away for a bit, he can't see us, but he gains strength from knowing that what he's doing helps us.

My dad is an old-fashioned guy in lots of ways. He says to me all the time that we, as men, should look after the women in our family over anything else, and he's brilliant at this. It sounds a little outdated maybe, and I don't doubt my mum and sisters could look after themselves (trust me, they've got it in them), but then when I see how other men of dad's age treat their wives and compare that to what my dad does, I realise how much good can come out of this. When I asked my mum about how Dad shows love, she said that it's in the way he takes care of everyone; the way he always leaves her a surprise in her lunchbox (even if it's just a little chocolate), puts a hot water bottle in the bed when she's coming back late from work, or gets up and de-ices everyone's cars on frosty mornings.

I think this comes from having a very strong view about what a man should be, and so he is old-fashioned in some respects, in that he's not always openly affectionate, but I know he's there for me when I need him. If I had something to share, I wouldn't hesitate to do so, because I know he can handle all aspects of people. And while I talk a lot about him working and how he went out every day to provide for the family, when he was unemployed, he put aside any pride and helped raise me and my brother for a little bit. I would say this makes him a very modern and incredibly manly man.

I would say my dad is the most passionate cook in our house, and he's always loved making meals for us. I remember one time when I was a kid, he roasted a chicken and put lemon on it for a bit of flavour. It didn't taste at all like the chicken I was used to. Now, I'm not only a fussy eater, I'm really stubborn too. My dad wanted me to eat a proper meal, but I refused to touch it, and so at 11 p.m., when it was really dark outside, there we were, sitting quietly at the dinner table, me still in my school uniform, each of us refusing to budge. (I guess I get my stubbornness from Dad, too.) Eventually, he gave me some Weetabix and sent me to my room. I think when I was sixteen, my parents just gave up trying to make me eat well.

My dad is a bit of a rule-breaker. He always says that rules are there to be broken, and I think he worries about that same boldness being in me. He would come to watch me play footie as a kid, as a centre-back (same position he played), and see that I never shied away from a challenge. Any ball was mine. No man was too big to bring down. I understand it might be concerning as a parent to see your kid run around and not worry that he might be getting on people's nerves, but I think of it as a strength. And so, when I read the Bible or went to church, I wouldn't get distracted by what other people thought or what the rules seemed to dictate; I would focus on what I thought about a Bible passage or an idea, and share what it meant to me. I'm going to talk about this in more depth later, but I want to say that what I believe is in no small part down to my dad.

And one of the biggest things I believe in (in a different way!) is Chelsea FC. It's something we've always shared, my dad and me, supporting Chelsea. George supports Liverpool, so we just think he's an idiot. As my dad says, there's only one colour, and it's blue, not red. Alfred, my younger brother, doesn't really have a team because he's into boxing, so mostly it would just be me and Dad sitting down to watch matches together. It was kind of our special thing.

As tickets to Prem games are so expensive and Dad never had the money to take all of us boys, we'd watch on the telly at home or in the pub, me in whatever kit I had, him in his old, battered one. Then, for my 10th birthday, he got me a ticket to Stamford Bridge to see Chelsea vs Everton. We travelled down by train a bit early, so we could meet the other lads in the pub (don't worry, I had a Coke). Dad asked for my advice on who was going to be the first goal scorer and put a bet on, and then we went to our seats. It was so exciting, being there, watching the players come out and hearing the crowd roar. Stamford Bridge is not a huge stadium like Old Trafford or The Emirates, so the sound's quite contained in the steep stands, and that means the noise is amazing.

At half-time, I wanted to get up and go to the toilet, but Dad wouldn't let me leave. I couldn't understand why and started complaining, when suddenly the big screen was illuminated with 'Happy 10th Birthday Harry Clark', and the whole crowd cheered! Everyone around was wishing me happy birthday, and I thought, 'This is what it must feel like to be famous.' It was amazing. Definitely one of the best moments of my life. I was so happy, and you could see Dad was too.

Just after *The Traitors*, I was invited by Chelsea FC to watch them play in the Carabao Cup Final at Wembley. It was incredible because they gave me tickets to the lounge before the game and let me bring a load of people. My family, my best friend and some cousins came, but really, it was great just to be able to give that to my dad. The truth is, he doesn't need special stuff; I think if you asked him, his favourite time with me would be us just randomly hanging out together. He told me recently that one of his fondest memories is when we went down to London, got a KFC and sat in the cinema together. He even remembers the film we watched (*Wind River*). But despite this, he was really excited when I told him we were going to the final.

A couple of hours before the game, we sat down to lunch. We were all at one big table, probably making more noise than the rest of the lounge combined. Not playing it cool at all. I look around and everyone's having a great time, tucking into their awesome food and getting served drinks by the waiters. Except for my dad. He's sat there, not smiling, just frozen, and I can see his head ticking, trying to work something out. So, I go over there, 'Dad, what's up?' 'Nothing, mate. I'm just wondering how much this bill is going to come to.'

The look on his face when I told him, 'Dad, we've been invited by Chelsea FC . . . as guests . . . it's all free.' The guy must have had two bottles of wine before kick-off. Not sure he even remembers what happened in the game.

But that's my dad. No matter what it would have cost him, no matter how hard he had to work to get the money, no matter how nervous he was about buying three courses and drinks for so many people, he would have done it for us. And I want to be like that with my family. He's always worried I'm going to turn out like him and is always telling me to better myself and not get as angry at things. (Last time he did that, it was in the car and about five seconds later, ironically, he was shouting at some guy who'd just cut him off!) And that's because he works incredibly hard and cares so much for us all.

My family's been through a lot, but we'll always find strength because we're always sticking together. One of the parts of our lives we're struggling with right now is that my grandad (my dad's dad, Allen) has dementia. It's a horrible disease, and it's sad to watch him sometimes, as he's not quite who he used to be, and gets confused a lot. When *The Traitors* was on the telly (and it is on quite a lot even now, as my nana loves to put it on and just watch it over and over again), he points at the telly and says, 'That's my son.' I guess he can see how similar me and my dad are. And that makes me really happy.

3
GRANDPARENTS

I'M LUCKY ENOUGH to have had all four of my grandparents around my whole life, which I know is not the situation for a lot of people. I see it as a blessing—I feel as if I've learnt something different from each one, and that's why I want to write about them here. They appear in no particular order, as I love them all equally, but seeing as I've already mentioned Grandad Allen, my dad's dad, I should probably start with him.

Grandad Allen taught me how to look cool. I don't want to make my other grandad sound unstylish, but Grandad Allen was always the one who had a white shirt popped open, chest hair out and his nice gold chain on show. He had slicked-back hair and smelled nice. (He has the best collection of aftershave ever; because of him, to this day, I always visit my own little aftershave collection before I go out.)

In a way, Grandad Allen was a bit like a mafia boss, always dressed up in a sharp shirt and pressed trousers, always clean-shaven whenever he left the house, even if it was just to the shops. I don't think he really did it to impress anyone; it just seemed to be his idea of what you should do to look good.

Whenever people tell me I look good, I feel as if I've drawn on Grandad Allen's sense of style. But he's influenced me in so many ways. He was the original footballer and Chelsea fan in the family. He played for Tottenham in his teens, and I think he must have been pretty talented, because he even had a few caps from one of the England national youth teams. There are quotes out there of people saying he was a great centre-back (again, as you can see, it's a family tradition). While he played for Tottenham, his cousin, Peter Osgood—known as 'The King of Stamford Bridge', for anyone who's not aware—played for Chelsea. Grandad Allen told me that, back in the day, he'd have to get up at three or four o'clock in the morning to get all the way over to North London for Tottenham matches. However, it was just one bus to Stamford Bridge in Fulham, so the family would go there every week to watch Peter play, and then they got into supporting the club, and that's how the Chelsea fandom started. After about ten years, Peter moved to Southampton (apparently, he fell out with the management at Stamford Bridge), and my family did go to watch him play there, but by then they were diehard Chelsea fans.

It's mad now to think just how much of a legend Peter is. He scored in every round of the FA Cup in 1970, and also in two cup finals during the following two seasons. When me and Dad went to Stamford Bridge, we walked past the statue of Peter next to the stadium as we were leaving, and that was a good moment. The statue was actually sculpted by Philip Jackson, who created the statues of Sir Bobby Moore and Sir Alf Ramsey outside Wembley Stadium, and of Sir Alex Ferguson and Sir Matt Busby at Old Trafford; he's even done memorials for The Queen Mother and Mahatma Gandhi. Apparently, Peter's ashes are buried under the penalty spot at the Shed end of Stamford Bridge. That's how much of a hero he was to Chelsea fans, my family included.

As I mentioned, Grandad Allen has dementia, and everyone is finding that really sad. It's the worst disease in the world and steals your loved ones away from you. I want to do as much as I can to help find a cure for it in my lifetime, whether that's taking part in big races, like the London Landmarks Half Marathon I ran last year to raise money for charity, or just generally increasing awareness and removing the stigma around the condition. It's terrible that it affects so many people, as family and friends have to watch the person with dementia change and struggle. How do we not know more about it? I feel like there must be something we can do. Grandad Allen is still with us and still loves to tell stories about Peter, as well as of his own days playing and especially his England caps, but with that horrible disease plaguing him, that's about all he can remember now.

When I was growing up, Grandad Allen would always be asking me about my football and how I was getting along. Sometimes he'd come to my games and watch me play, standing on the sidelines, chattering away to Dad, probably about what I should be doing or about Peter again. Most of the time I spent with Grandad Allen would be on Saturday nights, when I'd stay round at my grandparents' house, and this was when I found out just how much he was into fitness. Dad would drop me off, and when I walked in (with my Spider-Man suitcase in one hand and my PSP in the other), Grandad Allen would be in his boxers, sitting on an exercise bike, reading the horse racing section of the newspaper, right in the middle of their front room. Then he'd do a thousand sit-ups. So, he was proper into fitness before, I think, fitness was really a thing. Now, everybody goes to the gym, but back then, Grandad Allen was the standout one who always looked fit. He wasn't a posh kid (no one in my family's posh), but he grew up in quite a posh area, as I'm not sure Windsor's ever been rough. I think that's why he took care of himself so well; he wasn't rich, but he wanted to look good despite that.

I mean, it worked on my nana. Grandad Allen met Nana (or Lorraine, to him) when they were both young. I've never heard much more about their relationship than that, so I'm not really sure what Nana was like then. All I've got to go on is how she treated me. Unlike Grandad Allen, who was always a bit of a soft touch, focusing on his sit-ups, Nana is quite strict. She loves us all—she was the one who kept every single one of my newspaper clippings when I was on *The Traitors*—but she also wants us to be tough, and she doesn't take any prisoners.

I remember one time when I was around their house, I had a wobbly front tooth. It had been like that for weeks, and I loved wobbling that thing, though people would get really grossed out by it. Anyway, I was standing in the kitchen, holding my tooth with my fingers and wobbling it (maybe just for my own enjoyment) when Nana kicked my elbow so my hand shot forward and pulled the tooth right out. But that's the type of woman she is: tough, strong and sort of the protector of the family. When her grandparents (my great-grandparents) came over from Italy, they were living in caravans. I have photos of them, and they are the hardest-looking people in the world. I think my nana is scary at times, but the photo I've seen of *her* nana . . . well, she is the toughest-looking woman ever.

I reckon my dad gets his strong protector instinct from that side of the family. He and Nana are very similar in that, and because both of them know they have to look after everyone, they tend not to stress about things. My dad doesn't let a lot faze him, and neither does Nana. Nowadays, she's living her best retired life, as she and Grandad Allen are away a lot in Portugal, and we sometimes go with them. They love it there. I think it's the Italian in Nana that just loves the sun.

And what's great is that they've been happily married the whole time. Both sets of my grandparents are still together, and even though my grandads would probably tell you their wives are a pain in the ass (and Nana and Granny would probably say the exact same thing about them), they stick together. I'm grateful for that, and that my parents are still together, too. When I was growing up, a few of my friends' parents were separated and, being a cheeky kid, I was always jealous that they got two Christmases. I mean, come on . . . two sets of presents! When I complained, my parents would say, 'just be glad that you've got two parents who love each other', and they were right about that.

Now I'm older, I'm even more aware of how lucky I am. Divorce isn't anyone's first choice, but I support it if your marriage really isn't making you happy. No one on their deathbed is going to be saying they're glad they stayed in a terrible relationship because they were too afraid to get divorced. But I get the sense from talking to my parents that it's still not easy. Marriage can be difficult as you go through everything: house, kids, finances, jobs, mental health struggles, ups, downs, the whole of life, and it does take work. I believe you first need to be 100% certain that you've found your person for life (but we'll get onto Anna later) and then work hard to create something beautiful together.

I think one of the reasons my grandparents are happy is because of the family they've created. My Grandad Dave always makes a little speech about this at Christmas. He tells us that he's grateful to have us all sitting around the Christmas table for another year. He's grateful, too, that there haven't been any massive arguments, that no one has left the family, and that we're all still alive. It's a really great tradition.

It's funny to introduce my Grandad Dave with a story about him making a heartfelt speech, because he's not at all soppy and actually not much of a talker. He's a man of action, really. If Grandad Allen taught me how to look like a gentleman, Grandad Dave taught me how to act like one. I remember going down to the pub with him once when I was twelve (I had a Coke; don't come for me), and Grandad Dave showed me how to properly shake someone's hand. Firm grip and eye contact reveal confidence, but also trust and that you have strength in you, which I do now think is very important for all men. His sense of what an old-fashioned gentleman should do also extended to suits. Every year, my brothers and sisters and I would get a box of chocolates from him and Granny for our birthday, but when I reached twenty-one, they gave me my final present, a golden stopwatch to wear with a suit. It makes me look sharp, but it also reminds me to act like a gentleman.

When the producers of *Pilgrimage* asked if they could film me somewhere I spend a lot of time, I picked the boxing gym Grandad Dave owns, as it's one of my favourite places to be. In the introduction to the show, you can actually see us working with the pads, him telling me what to do and teaching me to keep my head down. It was a brilliant moment and really sums him up. Grandad Dave started the Jubilee Boxing Gym in 2008, when I was about seven, as a way of keeping kids off the streets and encouraging them to do something useful and meaningful. He was obviously aware of how easy it is for kids to fall into gangs and then start fighting in the wrong way, whereas boxing could give those same kids an outlet for their aggression and energy in a contained space. People tend to get things wrong about blood sports: they assume something like boxing makes you aggressive and ready to fight people in the real world, but, in fact, fighting in the ring means you actively avoid confrontation elsewhere, because you know you can handle yourself and don't need to prove anything. Grandad Dave always says, 'You should be a gentleman outside of the ring, but an animal inside it', and that's something I live my life by. And not to go into detail too early (we'll get there), that probably shaped my attitude in *The Traitors* . . . the second I got into that turret and put that cloak on, I was a Traitor, but then outside, I just switched into Faithful mode, almost telling myself that I really was a Faithful. People call it compartmentalising, where you store different parts of yourself in different parts of your brain, and I do feel I'm crazily good at that. It's my Jekyll and Hyde switch.

Some people may think that makes me a bit of a psycho, but I believe it's more like a discipline, one I definitely learnt from Grandad Dave. I began boxing in his gym when I was maybe eight or nine years old, and whenever we were working together, he always wanted me to give 110%. He'd tell me he didn't care whether I won or lost a contest: all he was concerned about was that I'd given my best. You would never get out of the ring and say, 'Oh, Grandad, I should have done this', or 'I should have thrown this', or 'I wasn't fit enough', or 'I wish I'd gone for that run two weeks ago' because he'd turn round and say, 'Well, why didn't you?' If you lost, he'd give you a hug and tell you to move on. And that was great, because I started to realise that if you want to get better at something, you've got to put everything in and keep trying. Move on to the next thing, and you'll get there.

That was another thing Grandad Dave taught me: the difference between cockiness and confidence. You can easily get the two muddled up, and I think many people do. What I learnt from him was that being cocky was walking into a situation and being arrogant about it to the point where you don't feel you need to improve. Confidence is knowing that you can do anything you set your mind to, but that it's going to take work. And boxing is the perfect thing to teach you these lessons, as if you don't put the work in, you get punched in the face. I love that these ideas are like seeds Grandad Dave planted in me to grow.

He never had a desk job because he has too much energy, and we're the same in that respect. I need to be doing something physical for most of my day. I remember talking to Grandad Dave about this when I was thirteen or fourteen, and when he asked me what I wanted to do after school, I said it was to be a professional football player or a professional boxer. And (probably because he'd seen I wasn't quite good enough at either) he replied, 'You do realise that you can do boxing and football in the Army and get paid for it?' He was in the Army himself, but no one in the family knew, because he never even mentioned it. (See, I told you he wasn't much of a talker.) Anyway, the second I heard that, I was in. I knew that was what I wanted to do, and, thankfully, he was able to tell me what it was like. But we'll get to the Army later.

While I got a lot—including some genuinely life-changing advice—from Grandad Dave, I got my sense of humour from

Granny (Bridget, to those not related to her). She's actually my dad's mother-in-law, but they get on like a house on fire. Whenever we have a barbecue, it's always those two standing in the corner laughing and gossiping away, she with a can of Foster's in her hand. Granny's always there if I ever need a chat, but she loves to talk, so if I call her in the evening, I admit I'll be thinking, 'If I ring her now, we'll be sitting here till past midnight'. When people meet her, I think they're surprised by how much chat and energy can be generated by such a small woman, because she's four foot nothing and weighs about thirty kilos.

She also has a huge amount of love in her, which is another thing I'm glad to have inherited. She cares so much for all her family and loves watching me on *The Traitors*. I think she's seen it six times now, all the way through. And that involves no small amount of work for me, because I have to teach my grandparents how to use the TV every single time they want to watch it on catch-up. Then Granny will obviously call all her friends to tell them I'm on the show, like they don't already know.

My dad calls her the Irish Witch, partly because she's a little crazy, but mostly because she has these weird premonitions. Each time we've had a new member join the family, she's guessed before it's been announced. My older cousin Ted found out he was having his first daughter, Emmy, but about two weeks before anyone else had heard about it, Granny had a feeling and rang my mum. 'Who's pregnant? Is it Harry? Is it George?' We all told her she was mad, but then Ted revealed his girlfriend was actually having a baby. Then, when my older brother George found out that my niece Daisy was on the way, Granny had a dream that someone in the family was pregnant, and it became a mystery until George made his announcement. And apparently these weren't the first . . . after my mum got pregnant with me, she walked into Granny's house and Granny said she 'smelt a baby'. The evidence of her abilities is starting to mount up. And so . . . the Irish Witch.

Granny is from County Mayo, so her family lived through the Irish potato famine, and I think a lot about how easily one of Granny's family members might not have made it. And if they hadn't made it, then Granny would never have been born, and she wouldn't have met my grandad, and they wouldn't have had my mum, and she wouldn't have met my dad, and I wouldn't exist. And then I feel incredibly grateful to be here. Obviously, I believe in someone watching over me and giving me what I need to get through, but when I consider that (like every person in the world today), I have literally thousands of ancestors, all of whom had to suffer hardship, pain and whatever life threw at them, had to bring up a family and keep that family alive through everything in order for me to be alive today, I find that pretty incredible. It makes me very happy to be here, and during times when I am feeling down, it certainly helps me keep things in perspective.

Obviously, Grandad Allen's struggling right now, but my other grandparents are quite old and frail too, and I definitely need to see them more. I do worry about giving them flu or any illnesses I might have had (which I'm sure concerns a lot of people after Covid), but when they've been in hospital, I haven't visited as much as I should. I hate hospitals, as there have been times in my life when I've been a patient myself and been in so much pain, so they just have bad vibes for me.

That's irrelevant, though, because I'm here due to my wonderful grandparents, not just physically, but in terms of where I am in my life. They've given me everything—their support, their advice, their stories, their passions, their humour, their personalities, their understanding and their love—and I will always appreciate that.

4

BROTHERS AND SISTERS

IN CASE IT'S NOT already obvious, my family are incredibly important to me, and my brothers and sisters play a big part in my life. I love them all so much. They're quite different from one another (and from my parents, too), and they could probably each have had a chapter to themselves, but then this book would be huge. Yet, it wouldn't be complete without them, as they helped shape who I am today. So, I'm going to stick them together here, each in their own section. They definitely didn't get to read what I'm saying first or make any comments, so you are getting the unvarnished truth.

George

I have two brothers, George and Alfred, and I'm really close to both of them. George is the oldest sibling by a few years and, as I mentioned, Mum had him before she met my dad, but we don't use the phrase 'step-son' in my house because, as far as my dad's concerned, he brought George up and has always regarded him as his own son. That's taught me a lot about family being the people you spend time with and care about, and look after.

As George was around for my entire childhood, we really were best friends growing up. I mean, we also sort of hated each other at the same time, though I think that's just a natural part of brotherly love. We're both competitive and passionate about boxing, and because he was bigger than me (not better, just bigger), he used to beat me up to teach me a lesson. I became aware that you need to watch out for guys who are bigger than you, but also that men can be tough and aggressive and, at the same time, very soft and sensitive. George would beat me up and then take the fall for anything I'd done, because he cared so much about me. I think I got away with loads of stuff because George didn't mind being my protector.

If you ask anyone who knows him, they'll tell you that the second he gets a couple of drinks down him, George will start talking non-stop about how much he loves everyone in our family. I went into the Army when I was sixteen, so I wasn't technically allowed to drink while I was there (how crazy is that). I remember coming back home just after I turned eighteen, and as I was finally of legal age, I went down to the pub with my family, my cousins and some of my old friendship group. I think I'd been away for a solid couple of months before this night out and started telling everyone about all the cool stuff that I'd done (at least, what the Army allowed me to talk about; they can understandably be strict about that). But though I was excited to share these great stories, they'd heard them all already! George had told them everything because he was just so proud of me.

It's great that he's started his own family now. Last year, he and his girlfriend Ashleigh had my niece Daisy, and she's the most beautiful thing ever. I'm really awkward around babies, because when they're born, they obviously don't do much—they don't react to you or smile or anything, they just lie there—but when I first saw Daisy, I couldn't stop smiling. In my head, I was like, this is the next generation of our family, and it's so cool. My cousins have had kids, and it's great, but Daisy's coming into the world really made an impact on me. I felt I would do anything for her, and I think that's unlocked something of my own desire to be a dad.

Anna and I have talked about this, so it's not like she's going to be in for a massive surprise when she reads here that I would like about ten kids. I would have started years ago, but Anna has her head screwed on a lot more than I do and has slowed me down. Plus, we both live with our parents right now, which is a bit of a dealbreaker, as we don't want to bring kids up while we're in that position. When we met, I think Anna wanted one or two children, whereas now she's agreeing to three or four, so I've slowly been getting the numbers up, but yeah, I can't wait to give Daisy loads of cousins. As I said, that's what I believe my purpose is: to be here, to have a family, to love them and to give them everything I've got. Then I can die a happy man. And just as I'm sure I'll love my kids more than life, I know George loves and will care for Daisy like nothing else. Looking at him that day when I first saw her, I knew he'd be a great dad.

My mum always calls me the rock of the family, but every rock needs its own rock, and George is mine. When you're growing up, you don't realise how much people do for you, but George was always there, and he's the person I continue to look up to. I will always keep trying to be a little bit nicer, a little bit better, a little bit more like my big brother.

Delilah

Age-wise, after George and me comes Delilah, two years younger and the maddest of the bunch. You can hear her from a mile away because she's so loud, but she does bring the vibes. She's always been exuberant and full of energy.

Delilah used to play guitar in the church band while I played violin, and then, as well as serving Mass on Sunday, we used to go on church retreats together. That's how we got close as kids, and (unlike my brothers) she didn't want to beat me up in the boxing ring. Now, she loves working and is a hair stylist in Ascot, but while she's doing that, she's also starting up her own company, Lilah's Locks, which sells extended hair rollers that let you curl your hair without tangles. I don't really know anything about this, as my luscious locks are natural, but I've heard it's a thing and am so impressed. She's making us all proud.

While George and I were genuinely best friends for a long time, when he moved into adulthood, he wasn't as up for socialising, so Delilah and I started going clubbing, and she was always great fun. I think our nights out on the town were when I started to realise how similar we are. She's like me in girl form: same cheeky smile, same desire to be the entertainer, same fearlessness. When I say fearlessness, I don't just mean that she's always the first to get on the karaoke mic; she is a risk-taker, which I am too. Everyone is scared of something, and if I said to you I didn't have any anxieties, that would be a massive lie, but I think we both try not to take things too much to heart. We know that if we don't push the fear away, compartmentalise it somewhere in our heads, it's going to stop us. So, we'll be first up on the dance floor; we'll do things like start businesses or go on reality TV shows, because we know that can get us where we want to be.

Delilah has a boyfriend who is actually my hairdresser. I go to him all the time, so I'm not sure what would happen if they broke up. (I'd either never get a haircut again or tell Delilah she has to learn how to cut my hair. I've cheated on one hairdresser before, and you don't do that twice.) But I hope they stay together because they make a great pair—like two peas in a pod, both really cool, and each just as loud as the other. Also, he treats her really well, and all that matters to me is that she's happy.

Finally, like me, Delilah loves kids. She's Auntie Lilah to Daisy and wants a big family of her own one day. As I said, like me in girl form. I don't know when that will happen; she and her boyfriend aren't married yet (and I'm not going to talk about sex before marriage in the context of my sisters), but what I do know is that is going to be one loud house.

Alf the Great

When Delilah began to get more absorbed in her work and business, I started going out on the town with Alf. Clearly, I'm the problem; the only one who's not grown up! But I couldn't pass up the chance of going out with Alf. If George is my idol, Alf is my mini-idol. His name's Alfred, but we all call him Alf the Great, with good reason. I honestly think that if people could be more like Alf, the world would be a nicer place. He's basically the best of me and the best of George put together. (I think he's learnt from our mistakes.)

It's actually quite hard to describe why we all love Alf so much, but maybe that's how it sometimes works with family.

He's the most chilled-out guy ever, and I just love spending time with him. We game together, and I'm not sure he quite realises it, but that's the way I de-stress. Whenever I have a busy day, all I want to do is get to my room, sit down, jump on with the boys and play some games. We'll sit there and chat, moaning about how someone's just killed us or generally beat us at the game, or talking about what he's got up to during the day or what we're doing that weekend. Sometimes we'll speak about bigger life matters. He'll tell me how things are in the Army, because he's joined, working as a cybersecurity engineer, and I'll tell him about whatever's going on with me that week (which could be anything). And when he's back from the Army, we'll sometimes sit together and watch YouTube videos on how to upgrade our base quicker on *Clash of Clans* (we're in the same clan, obviously) or of someone dropping the kill record on *Call of Duty*. We are such massive nerds, but, like my dad says, we're also just mates, and that's really nice.

It's fun to compete with my brothers at anything, and recently we really got into padel (a racquet sport) and often go down to the local courts with our mates to battle it out. But it's annoying playing against Alf because he's so good at everything. Even though he can't admit it, I'm better at *Call of Duty* (there, that's in print now), but one thing I'll never be better at than Alf is boxing. He started at my grandad's gym when he came of age, though he wasn't really a boxer; he much preferred football. Then, I think he started to realise how agile he is and how much that can be an advantage for him in the ring. He always says I got Dad's height, while he's a bit shorter, and is annoyed by that, but it makes him so quick when he's boxing, and he's become the Armed Forces Champion. He actually won the army championships two years in a row, which is so cool. Hopefully, he'll go to the Olympics one day, but whether he does or not, we are all so proud of him. Alf the Great, ladies and gentlemen.

Matilda

Matilda is the youngest, and I feel like I want to do everything to protect her. I want her to succeed, I want her to thrive, and I want her to be happy. If I ever have a bit of cash lying around, I'll just give it to her, like I'm her Tooth Fairy or something, although I'm not really sure she needs that much help. She is technically the baby of the family, and I think we all want to keep treating her like that, but Matilda's also almost like the mum of the family, too. She's the most mature 17-year-old I've ever met in my life and is ten years ahead of her time. One of the ways this is obvious is in how she puts time and energy into what she's passionate about, and really sticks with it. She knows that's how you create a good life and find happiness and contentment.

Every morning, without fail, she gets up at 5 a.m. to go where her horse is stabled. She'll have a ride, then pet and feed the other horses, and she absolutely loves it all. When she's taking part in a show-jumping competition, the whole family will go and support her. Mum actually used to be a show-jumper (Delilah too until she got injured) and has loads of trophies, so she knows about the life and they share that together. Matilda's also doing Equestrian Studies at college, so it's not just a hobby, and I think she's thinking seriously about veterinary school when she's old enough.

Unfortunately, I'm really allergic to horses, so while I'd love to support her in this part of her life, every time I've been to that stable yard, I'm in pain for at least a couple of hours afterwards. My eyes get itchy, my nose feels terrible, and everything just shuts down. For the episode of *The Traitors* when we were acting out Diane's funeral, they brought in horses for the procession, and it was awful. For hours afterwards, I could barely speak. I don't know how they managed to edit together the turret scene because after every other word, I would do a massive sneeze, and my eyes were bulging out of my head. Paul was wetting himself laughing. But also, have you ever seen a horse? They're huge. Really big and so strong. I feel that if one wanted to run you over, they could do so without thinking. Basically, I've decided that I only like horses when they're winning me money.

I do wish I could share in Matilda's passion because the age gap has meant we can't really go out much together. However, recently she's started asking for my advice on joining the Army, either as a vet or as a combat medic. Combat medics are right in the heart of any danger going on, and she's my baby sister, so I don't know if I'd feel too happy about that. But I also understand that you can't stop someone from doing what they really want to do. Maybe, like me and Lilah, she's a bit of a risk-taker; maybe she's just after adventure. She's spoken to us all numerous times about how she'd love to go out to Bondi Beach in Australia and become a lifeguard. But if you asked me what I think Matilda will be doing in the years to come, I honestly couldn't tell you. She's such a hard worker, she could turn her hand to anything. I do know that I'll be there to support her. And maybe slip her a little cash too.

As I mentioned at the start of this chapter, my brothers and sisters didn't get to read their own sections before this book was published, as my interest here is my relationship with them, rather than how they'd like to be written about. Ultimately, a family is just a collection of individuals interacting with one another, so I think you get a lot from hearing what someone you love thinks of you.

But one thing I did ask them about, because it's something I want to keep focusing on, is their relationship to religion. And their answers were really varied. George doesn't have a strong faith any more; Delilah doesn't go to church as often as she'd like; Alf has learnt to pray when he needs guidance; and Matilda sees God in the world around her. Despite coming from the same family, having the same parents and all going to church together when we were younger, every one of my siblings has a different viewpoint. And I do think that's what faith should be—one unifying belief that people interpret in their own ways. In that sense, it's not that different to a family.

5

HOW MY FAITH BEGAN

GOD HAS BEEN IN MY LIFE since I was born. I was baptised at the church literally round the corner from where we live, Our Lady of Peace. That church has a rich history in my family, because not only were my brothers and sisters and I baptised there, but it's where both my granny and grandad *and* my mum and dad got married. So, it's a really special place for all of us.

I'm not going to lie, though. When I was younger, I didn't love going there. Like I said, my mum would take us to church every Sunday, all dressed in our best, and we'd sit and listen to the Mass. But when you don't know really what the gospel story is, and you're too young to understand what it means and what it's telling you, I think it's hard to feel a part of things. The long lectures, the droning organ, the lack of special effects . . . it all kind of flew over my head.

But there was a high spot for me: the nativity play. That was organised by my school, which was a Catholic school attached to the church, and I'd always be so excited. I remember one year coming home and Mum asking me which part I got, and I told her I'd got the best one. Of course, she's hoping for Joseph (I think every parent wants their kid to be the main player in school performances), and she's standing there in the kitchen, with her fingers crossed that I'm the lead in the church play, or at least that I have a big role and maybe even some lines. And I'm jumping around, so excited because I'm going to be the donkey and I get to give Mary a piggyback across the stage! For me, it was the coolest thing ever, and I was so happy. I'm not so sure about my mum.

But though I struggled with church at the start, things changed when I got old enough to join the children's groups they ran, which was when I was about five or six years old. The church was really keen to speak to kids in the kind of language we could understand, so they would have little bits of teaching with music and drums to make it more entertaining. There were also times when we could sit around and have a conversation about the Bible, which was so much better for me than being preached at. I loved the children's groups; they were wicked. Looking back, I really appreciate how hard the church worked to create a space where you didn't get bored and didn't actually feel like you were being forced to sit through a Mass. The result, of course, was that you were much more likely to enjoy attending: you were getting to meet your mates and, as the years went by, growing up with these people and getting to know them better.

One of the biggest switches for most young kids in the Catholic faith is preparing for Confirmation around the age of fourteen. Unlike your parents baptising you or making you have Holy Communion, your confirmation is about you choosing to make a commitment on your own. So, you begin to look at things in more depth and start going to Bible classes. Usually, I'd sit there with a few other kids who were also preparing for their confirmation, and we'd go through a passage of the Bible before talking about it together.

I used to really love this. I loved talking about the Bible and explaining my own interpretation of it, though I think my answers sometimes came as a bit of a surprise to the teacher and my classmates. The best example I can think of was when we were discussing Adam and Eve (this was probably Day One, as it's pretty basic stuff). So, we read about Adam and Eve being the first people in the Garden of Eden and the snake tempting Eve and ruining everything (sorry for the spoiler). Then came the one question you're obviously going to get from a bunch of teenagers . . . 'Miss, if there's just one man and one woman who we all came from, doesn't that mean we're all inbred?' (Cue everyone feeling grossed out about us all being cousins.)

Anyway, when this question popped up, I said to the teacher that I thought I had the answer, and she asked me to explain. I said it seemed to me that it was a story, simplified for us to understand. Adam is a representation of man, Eve represents women, and the snake represents all the bad temptations in life. And the story is a warning about what happens to you if you choose to go down the path of being a horrible person and acting in evil ways. But the story also tells us that the Garden of Eden is what we're destined for, and if you live life without falling for the temptations of the snake, then the Garden can be where you end up. And everyone seemed pretty blown away by that.

My mum said that the teacher rang her after class and asked if she was in the habit of going through the Bible with me, but I'd never read the Bible before I went to those classes. The response I'd shared was based on my outlook on life. I try not to go too deeply into why I think something, and I guess that's partly down to my dad. He sees Bible teaching as a series of lessons that are supposed to make you a better, kinder person, and I've taken that into my faith, too.

I do feel people interpret the Bible too literally sometimes. After all, the earliest accounts (which are in the first part, the Old Testament) come from stories and poetry that have been handed down by word of mouth from one generation to the next for a very long time. (The second part of the Bible, the New Testament, is about Jesus's life and ministry.) Things can change and evolve in the telling. They certainly do in our family . . . I remember one time I went fishing with my dad. Beautiful day, calm breeze, and so nice being seated next to the canal. In the first hour, I managed to catch a fish (amazingly because that never tends to happen with me), and I instantly texted my mum. Naturally, I exaggerated a little and told her it was a decent size and that we were going to bring it home for dinner. In fact, it was the size of my palm, and I threw it back straight away, but by the end of the day, when I was telling the tenth person about this one tiny fish, it had become a monster. I had to use both hands to pick it up, and it strained my muscles to hold it as the scales glistened like a disco ball in the morning sun! But that's natural; that's just how stories change and evolve over time (though mine happened over the space of a single day, with my dad chuckling in the corner as I regaled everyone in the family with my heroic tales). It's almost weird not to bear this in mind when thinking about the Bible, which was written in very different times from our own.

I know we live in an age of Instagram, where people think a lot about themselves, but it feels almost selfish to me to assume that what you get out of reading the Bible—which was written for millions of people—is what everyone else should get out of it too. When I'm reading, I always try to see the lessons the stories are teaching me and then use them to help me in my life. A lot of the time, the lesson seems to be about being nice to people. That may not be everyone's interpretation, but as it has generally been part of my upbringing to be as kind as possible to everyone I meet, it's not surprising that it affects how I read the text.

Faith is different for every single person because no two people are the same. If you see things similarly to the way I do, then that's sick, but if you don't, that's just as cool. Who is to say what forms of faith are wrong and which are right? I would never try to change someone's beliefs, or their own personal reading of texts like the Bible, because that is theirs and theirs alone. I may never fully understand their personal interpretation of the text, but I can still respect how sincere their interpretation may be. I think if everyone was accepting of such differences and allowed that people may simply not believe what they believe, then there would be no arguments, no fighting and no wars. And that's what we should really be aiming for.

The Catholic faith has always been part of who I am, but I've never stopped exploring and questioning my beliefs. Last year, my agent told me they'd had an email from the producers of a BBC show, *Pilgrimage*, in which celebrities of different faiths go on a journey together. For this series, we'd all be trekking 3,000 km along a revived Catholic medieval route, the Austrian Camino, which would take us through the Austrian and Swiss Alps to Lake Zurich. The second the invitation came in, I knew I wanted to accept it, and the second I was confirmed for it, I started to do research on every other religion my fellow pilgrims practised. I knew I'd be spending time with these people and discussing their faiths, and I wanted to be able to put myself in their shoes and get where they were coming from. I was excited, not only to understand their beliefs better, but my own too. I'm going to go into more depth later about *Pilgrimage* and what it brought me at that time in my life, but one thing that it really highlighted to me was how many similar concepts are shared by different faiths.

To take one example, a lot of religions have, as part of their teachings, strong ideas around bad deeds, and many seem to suggest that you're damned for eternity if you put even one foot wrong. I recognise this in the Christian faith. To me, though, that feels ridiculous and not very accepting of the flawed nature of human beings. How could you go through life worrying that you may have ruined your life if you swear, or act in a nasty way or mess up, which we all do multiple times? Sometimes I feel people move away from religion, because it doesn't seem to allow for the varied behaviour of human beings. I don't want to excuse terrible deeds and behaviour, but I think people are just people, making mistakes, and if you apply individual action to broader concepts, that can cause a lot of confusion. After all, there are bad people in every religion, and there are good people who sometimes do bad things.

When Pope Francis died in April 2025, I got invited onto a few shows to talk about him and the Roman Catholic faith in general. I was sad that he'd passed away, because he did a lot of great things. And so, when I sat on those sofas, I said that, even though I was excited to see what the next Pope brings, I thought it was brilliant to have had a head of the church who had been such a good example to the world and the good that religion can inspire. All the same, there were a lot of scandals in the church while Francis was Pope, and in one of the interviews, I was asked how I can stay committed to my faith when there have been so many terrible deeds done in recent years. This subject comes up a lot when people are talking about religion, but the way I see it, it's got nothing to do with religion at all. I don't believe you can reject faith because of the mistakes, even if they are truly awful, of a few human beings

I suppose you could think of rather judgemental views like these as an extension of how some people interpret the Adam and Eve story: that is, literally. We read about Eve taking a bite of an apple and damning the whole of the human race, and assume that this translates to the real world—that one mistake, one sin, causes the world to crumble and morality to be completely lost. But faith is there for individuals to take and interpret as they need to, and some people act in better and worse ways than others.

I think that, even when I was a kid, I've thought of church as something we carry within us, rather than an organisation we follow. I get a lot of people in my faith (and outside it) who tell me that I'm not Roman Catholic because I don't go to church on Sunday. But, as I've mentioned, I believe I can practise my faith just as sincerely by praying at the end of my bed as I can sitting in a pew once a week. Obviously, listening to scriptures and gospels and singing hymns can make it easier to connect with why you're there, but sometimes I just can't make it, and sometimes I prefer to look the scriptures up to read them myself. It can even make me feel closer to God, knowing I have this personal connection to explore any time I want, rather than being bound to practising my religion for a few hours, once a week.

Life was so different when the Bible and the teachings of many major religions were written down. I don't want to invalidate what these teachings are or suggest that the Bible and the Ten Commandments aren't useful to people, but I feel we do need to take account how thinking has changed. The Bible is interpreted by some people as saying that we should stone gay people, but I definitely don't believe that. (It also says to love all of God's children, but that's a whole wormhole it's not worth getting into.) I think the idea that we need to keep engaging with the text and how it speaks to us today makes me quite a modern Catholic, but if being modern means loving everyone the same, then I'm proud to be so.

I was still a kid when I learnt that there's more to religion than just sitting, praying and discussing the Bible. The best thing the church brought into my life, without a doubt, came about through Lux Nymo.

Nymo (Northampton Youth Ministry Office) is an organisation that arranges events and support for kids, teens and young adults to help them discover and grow in their faith, and they do these long retreats that were so cool. When the summer holidays hit, I would spend the first two weeks basically with all my mates who I'd met through church. The retreats gave you time to talk about faith, and there was the same openness as in my church groups to express what things meant to you. But we'd also be playing football and doing climbing, and going to Alton Towers together. A typical day would start with breakfast, then we'd talk about scripture, and this would involve some fascinating questions, like: How do we live life in the best way possible? What can we do to become better? How do we become the best version of ourselves? And then after that, we'd be asked: Who wants to go mountain biking? So, we were talking about the Bible, but also just enjoying ourselves, spending time together and learning from one another. I feel it can be easy to underestimate the sense of community and enjoyment you can get through religion. A lot of people assume that being sent away to learn about faith must be a really serious thing, but actually, it can be about having great times with great people. The weeks at those retreats, which were some of my happiest ever, definitely showed me that.

Religion has also taught me about the importance of helping others. Through my church, I've done a lot of charity work, which has been really fulfilling. One year, I slept on the street for a night in order to raise money for an organisation that supports homeless people. I remember it was December, so it was freezing, and apart from a mat and a sleeping bag, we weren't allowed anything else to lie on. As the night wore on, I kept adding layers—an extra jumper, an extra pair of gloves, an extra three pairs of socks—until eventually I was wearing all the clothes I'd brought. I had a hot chocolate and I remember it tasting great (who doesn't love hot chocolate?), but being disappointed it didn't warm me up a lot more (I could probably barely feel it through my double-gloves). And even though it felt like a relief when I got into my sleeping bag, being on the cold, hard ground was tough, and no matter which way I turned, I wasn't comfy, and I did not sleep well at all. It made me feel compassionate towards the people who have to do this regularly, and I want to help them even more.

There's a lot of harsh judgements around people who sleep rough—that they must be drug addicts or be to blame themselves for ending up homeless—but I don't think we ever truly know people's circumstances. Life is difficult for everyone right now, with the cost-of-living and housing crises in the UK, and then all the terrible things that are happening in the rest of the world, and I think we need to remember that you can never guess what the person to the left or right of you is having to deal with. If someone charges you the wrong amount in a shop, or forgets your order, or makes a mistake at work (or has a go at you for doing any of these things), what might have caused them to act this way? They may have just received some terrible news or had someone close to them pass away, or be struggling generally with their mental or physical health.

What I learned from the church is to approach these situations from a place of kindness. We're all trying our best, and everyone has the capacity to be nice to those around them. I would say I'm a more compassionate and loving person because of things I've been led to do through my faith, and I'm so grateful to have it in my life. When I went through events that almost caused me to despair (more of which later), it really gave me something to hold on to.

One of the best moments from my childhood was my confirmation because I got to choose my saint. I picked Saint George, the slayer of dragons, because he was a soldier and a warrior, and I knew that's what I wanted to be. I didn't realise then that I'd be going into the Army, but I was sure I would fight for the things I cared about, and I still do believe that. I joined so that if we go to war, my family don't have to; they can be at home and be safe. I was given a sovereign coin at my confirmation of Saint George, and now I wear it proudly as a sovereign ring on my hand. You can see it glinting at you from *The Traitors* round table.

But while Saint George was my choice, my family had another. When I went away to the Army, they presented me with a coin on a necklace of Saint Christopher, the patron saint of travel. They gave it to me to keep me safe. And I really needed it for the journey I was about to undertake.

6

SCHOOL, SPORT AND FRIENDS

I THINK I'VE BEEN cheeky my whole life. 'Cheeky trouble', my parents call it. Basically, just always being a bit naughty and trying to get away with as much as I can. If you ever want to understand how I became the Harry who won *The Traitors*, just look at my time in school.

From the age of four, I attended Our Lady of Peace Catholic Primary and Nursery School, which, as I've mentioned, was really close to our house. One of the best things about it was that my whole family had gone there (and continues to go), so I pretty much had a cousin in every year. That meant I was never alone, which was great as I hate being alone, and also that I was always protected. My cousin Floss in the year above me was my absolute hero and saved me from ever being picked on.

I was still always trying to look hard, though. For example, I never used to sing the hymns we had in assemblies; I just used to stand there, thinking it made me look like a big man. That did get me in trouble, but I felt that rules were there to be broken, and so I'd always be pushing the boundaries. Not with things that would hurt other people, like bullying them or being mean to teachers, or anything that could get me expelled, like cheating on tests or stealing. I'd just do things I thought I could get away with—going to the loo five minutes before the end of class to get out early, or not doing my homework by saying my dog ate it (classic). The maddest excuse I used was that one of my grandparents had died. Obviously, no one checked if it was true because I never got pulled up, which meant I could produce the same excuse another three times!

I found out quite early on in school that I was great at coming up with stuff on the spot, but then my dad's always had a silver tongue. I've seen him throw out some mad excuses, like he would tell my mum that he'd done the vacuuming or cleaned the toilet when he totally hadn't. And if he ever got caught out, he would explain to her that he'd started but then someone from the doctor's surgery had rung and he'd had to have a long chat with them. About what? He'd have an answer to that, too. This is probably not a good look for my dad, but I think I learnt a lot from watching him, especially about thinking on my feet.

As soon as the teacher asked why my homework wasn't done, I would say whatever came into my mind. I've always believed that if you don't overthink something, then you put yourself in a much better position; you're not trying too hard, and what you say doesn't come out as too practised. Also, you can move and shift based on the response you get, whereas if you've planned everything out, when things don't go as you anticipate, you're stuck in the mud: scared and unable to move. There were people on *The Traitors* who'd watched the first season five or six times, and they'd mapped out their whole game based on what they thought would happen. I think that's where they slipped up and why things started to go downhill for them. I never sat down the night before and thought, 'If this person says this to me, then I'll respond like that,' because then if they didn't ask me the exact question I'd planned for, or if they found something else to throw at me, then I'd be like, 'Well, what do I do now?', and start to panic.

However, although I think it's better not to have a script to follow, I do believe you can have a goal to aim for, as long as you're prepared for the route to follow a squiggly rather than a straight line. I've always taken comfort in telling myself that I'm never quite sure how I'll get to what I want, but I know I will get there. I guess that's my faith.

This can apply to anything in life. Say you wanted to have kids by the time you were twenty-five, but, for whatever reason, that didn't happen (maybe you broke up with your partner, maybe you couldn't get pregnant when you'd planned), then you're going to feel like you've failed and potentially even give up. But the end goal of having children is still there, and you can still achieve it, just maybe not in the way or within the timeframe you thought. My end goal with *The Traitors* was to win the money, and I kept that in mind throughout, but I didn't know *how* winning would happen, and so I just took everything, all the shifts and surprises and betrayals, as they came.

My ultimate aim with school was to get out as soon as possible. I hated being there; I just had too much energy. I wanted to play football, to box, to run around, and compared to those things, school was just so boring. I do remember my older cousins telling me that they wished they could go back to school and that one day I'd feel the same. They said it was basically daycare for kids; that it wasn't the real world, and that not having any bills to pay or other grown-up things to stress out about was great. I can see where they were coming from now, and I would totally go back if I could, but at the time, I just couldn't wait to be an adult. I wanted to work and to make money, and to become a man.

I never understood how algebra or trigonometry was going to help me in my life. Whenever I'd visited my dad on the building site, I saw people doing a good job and making money without that stuff, so why was I bothering? For work experience, I was taken on by my local butchers, and they had me making them cups of tea and chopping up garlic and herbs and scrubbing the dried blood off the floors of the walk-in fridge. I remember sometimes my head would touch the meat hanging from the ceiling, and whatever juices were dripping from it would get into my hair and make it really crispy for the rest of the day, until I could get home and wash it out. And still, I preferred this to school. I thought I was smarter than everyone else, because I'd worked out you could get paid without any knowledge of physics or maths.

That's why joining the Army seemed so attractive. I wouldn't have to go to sixth form or uni; I could dispense with Pythagoras' Theorem and be getting money for my skills instead. And so, when I was fifteen and a half, I went to the Army assessment centre; the second I turned sixteen and I'd finished my GCSEs, I could be on my way.

One of the coolest things I've ever done is go back to my school to speak to the kids there after I won *The Traitors*. I noticed they had a photo of me in a frame in the cafeteria, next to all the other people from the school who've done great things. It seemed surreal! They took me into the headteacher's office and I looked around and thought about how I was in there, basically every other day, for being a bit naughty. I didn't love school, I think it just didn't suit me, but it did teach me how to lie, and that has changed my life for the better.

Obviously, though, I didn't tell the kids that.

There was, at school, one teacher who I liked and one class that I loved, and that was PE. All I've really cared about most of my life is playing sports, and the only hour that didn't go slowly was PE. If anything, knowing I had PE at the end of the day would make the rest of my classes drag. I was just so unfocused; I couldn't sit still; I couldn't read a book, and my foot was constantly tapping under the desk.

Just as I couldn't wait for PE, I couldn't wait for break time so I could play footie. As you know by now, my mum always wanted us to look smart, and she probably hated the fact that I was one of those kids who'd come home with holes in their school trousers from slide-tackling on the concrete. Fortunately, because my cousins had already been pupils, there would always be clothes getting handed down, but that did mean that in Year 7, when I started secondary school, I was wearing a blazer that basically went down to my ankles. It was honestly the biggest blazer in the world.

Anyway, I loved sport so much that I would get up early for it. Every morning, me and my best friend, Harry Brown (or Brown, as I call him), would be out of bed at 6 a.m. and we'd ride our bikes down to our secondary school so we could be in the gym by 6:30 a.m. and then we'd play basketball together. No matter how sunny it was outside or how freezing it was in the gym, we'd be there every day, pushing the ball up towards the net with our spindly arms. Brown is just as competitive as I am, so it got quite heated. And that wasn't limited to basketball; we were always competing—at footie, at rugby, at cricket, at tennis, we even tried American football together too.

I think once you become a sporty kid, that's all you care about. Playing sport improves your hand-eye coordination, and you learn that you can sort of pick anything up as you go along. Last Christmas, I got invited to a padel event (as I've mentioned in passing). I'd never played before, but I loved it. Afterwards, I told my boys that we had to go together, and at first they were like 'No, I ain't doing that', but then they tried it and that was it. Now we pretty much play every single night together, me and my best lads: Brown, Cole and Brad.

I should say that, although the best thing to come out of school was meeting Harry Brown, our friendship had a slightly unpromising start.

We met in Year 6 at a football tournament, where my school was playing his. We smashed his team, and I scored about six goals; I think I even scored an overhead kick. Afterwards, this guy came up to me and said, 'Good game', and told me we were actually going to be at the same school the next year. I said, 'Yeah, alright mate', like, we're not going to be friends, and I was thinking that Our Lady of Peace was my school, not his. But then the next year, we're both in Year 7, we're both called Harry, which we thought was cool, and suddenly we're joined at the hip.

Now, he's not only my closest friend but almost like another brother to me. People call us 'The Harry and Harry Show', like Ant & Dec, but with worse jokes . . . Once, for my sister Delilah's 21st birthday party, we really leaned into it. Because we both love to have fun and entertain other people, you know that when you come to the Harry & Harry

Show, you're going to have a great time. We walked into the party, arm-in-arm, wearing the same multi-coloured sparkly rainbow suit, the loudest suit you've ever seen in your life, and people weren't shocked at all. Everyone, especially my relatives, was like, We expect nothing less.

We're quite similar in that we both love our families, both love sport and are both very competitive. We argue all the time over who's better at what. He'll say he's better than me at football, which he's not. And our mates agree, so it must be true (but it's still so annoying that he won't shut up about it). He thinks he's better at padel, which is also wrong. I'm definitely better than him at pub games, particularly darts. The only thing he may be better at than me is golf, but golf is the perfect sport for him because he's just so relaxed, and you can't really be a stressed-out golfer who just whacks it (like me) and be any good.

I tell him everything because he's the least judgemental character ever. If you want to get something off your chest, Brown's your man and, luckily, he's my shoulder to cry on when I need one. I'll also run anything by him and will frequently ask him if he thinks I'm being a dick with doing this or that, and I trust him, because I feel like we're close enough that he knows what I'm dealing with and can put me on the right path.

Even though we are similar, they say that opposites attract, and we are also quite different in some ways. I always say I'm the fighter and he's the lover. He's the most chilled-out person in the world, whereas I'm a bit mental. He's happy just doing whatever job he's doing and going home, whereas I want more than that. So, I'm the massive dreamer, and I want to be able to give everyone I know the best life, whereas he's very content with what he has. I think Brown was the only friend who wasn't jealous when I won *The Traitors*—he was just happy for me. And I think that's because he doesn't care about the money or the fame. All he cares about is me being his friend, Harry. This keeps me grounded and reassures me that, even if I end up living underneath a bridge, if I have my family, Anna and Brown there with me, I'll be happy.

One thing Brown and I don't regularly chat about, and which we don't precisely agree on, is religion. I'm big into religion, and he's not, which is funny because I think he would tell you that he's witnessed me do the most unholy stuff he's ever seen! But that's just because he's known me in every type of situation you can imagine. He was kind of just going through the motions at our school, and I knew this, but he did say the nicest thing about faith when his nan passed away. He said that because she believed so much, when she was going, she was so peaceful because there was no fear there at all.

While we've never really sat and talked about God, we could talk for hours about who built the pyramids, and whether it was actually humans or giants or even aliens. You can ask Brown his thoughts on this, but I think the pyramids were built by a civilisation that had technologies beyond our understanding that are now lost to history. A bit like Greek Fire, an ancient and powerful military weapon used by the Roman Empire, which would continue to burn on and even under water, so it was known to be as psychologically damaging as it was physically destructive to your enemies. But any records of this have disappeared, and we still, to this day, don't know how it was made.

I should say that I also believe in aliens, and in a book about my faith, it feels as if this should be addressed, because people frequently tell me that I can't be Catholic and believe in aliens at the same time. My reasoning is that if there are aliens and life on other planets, that only shows how amazing God's creation is. He hasn't only created Earth and human beings, he's created a whole vast network and universe of life.

The more we understand about the vastness of the universe, the more crazy it feels that we're here, living out our days. The insane possibility of the Big Bang happening as perfectly as it did, with us eventually coming out of it as perfectly as we have—which is maybe one in a trillion, but probably even slimmer odds—only proves to me that there must be something else, a greater force at work. Because with friends like Brown, I can't be this lucky just by chance.

7
THE ARMY: EARLY DAYS

LIKE ALL 12-YEAR-OLDS when they begin secondary school, I was encouraged to start considering what I wanted to do with my life. At that stage, I had no idea—all I could think of was boxing and playing football. I felt kind of lost, to be honest, and no one really had any answers for me. Until, that is, Grandad Dave told me what the Army had to offer. Suddenly, I was imagining myself running around a field, shooting guns, being a soldier and doing all the sports I loved—all while getting paid for it. It sounded like a dream come true, and from that moment on, there was no continuing at school, no staying in Slough . . . it was set in stone: I was going to join the Army.

I think my mum was quite anxious about the idea of me going into the military. I mean, who would want their son on the front line with everything you hear on the news? But that stuff was exactly what I wanted to be a part of. I'd played *Call of Duty* for years and watched the Rambo movies with my dad. I wanted to be Harry Rambo! My grandad was a paratrooper, and I'd heard that they were the ones who parachuted behind enemy lines and got involved in hand-to-hand combat. I loved boxing and figured it used the same skills, so that all sounded sick.

My mum's always said that she doesn't care what we do, she just wants us to be happy. So, though she was scared,

I knew that she and Dad would support me, and after our conversation (which wasn't much of a conversation as I was so set on this next step), I got my parents' signature and set a date to go to the assessment centre.

The youngest you can be when you attend is fifteen and a half, six months before you turn sixteen, so that's exactly when I went. I was only a teenager, just a kid really, but I was keen to get on with becoming a man, and if I got through the tests, I could join the Army as soon as possible.

On the day of the assessment, I was really nervous. When you get there, they put you all in a line and shout at you to try and scare you into leaving. If you survive that, you stay the night in a twelve-man dorm, and early in the morning, you have to be up, washed and fully prepped for inspection, in fresh clothes and having made your bed with hospital corners. I realise that this sounds like some people's nightmare, but I loved it. The nerves were officially gone; I knew this was what I wanted to do.

The rest of the assessment consists of you being put through a load of tests: fitness tests, mostly just some running, and mental tests, including theoretical questions designed to see how well you can problem solve. Once you've finished all those, you go in for your final meeting. As I entered the office, I remembered what my grandad had taught me about sitting up straight, having my feet flat on the floor and my hands on my knees. I was worried there would be details that would let me down, but the second I got in there, the recruiter told me I'd smashed it and genuinely got the highest score possible. I asked, 'Does this mean I can be a paratrooper?' and they told me, 'Definitely. You can be whatever you want.' Then the recruiter stood up, shook my hand and welcomed me into the Army.

When I got home, I was glad to find that my parents were happy for me, and then I spent a week telling everyone at school I was going to be a paratrooper. However, about two weeks after my assessment, I got a call from the Army's career advisor. 'We hear you're joining the Army. Well done. Congratulations.' I said thank you. I was loving this. And then the advisor asked, 'Are you sure you want to be a paratrooper?' I was quite surprised, so I asked what they meant. 'Well, you've scored the highest you can on our tests, which means you can do anything. Are you sure you don't want to get a trade? Then, in case you get injured, you can come out and use those skills.' My response, as you can imagine, was 'Absolutely not.' I told them I couldn't care less about having a trade—I wanted to jump out of helicopters and planes. Then they asked to speak to my mum, who took the phone and immediately kicked me out of the room.

She was in there for twenty minutes, and when she came out, she told me that she'd heard about the advantages of getting a trade—you move up the ranks faster, you make more money, and you have a lifetime skill you can use outside the Army in a range of jobs. It's basically like getting a free education, except it isn't only free, you're being paid to acquire your skill. She'd asked which was the hardest course, and they'd said that Avionics Technicians have only an 11% pass rate. Apparently, if I passed Avionics, I'd have an NVQ Level Three in Aeronautical Engineering and could come out and work on anything: planes, helicopters, trains. So, she told them I was doing that.

With time, I'd learn to thank her. Not only was she thinking about my future, she was showing how much she believed in my ability to do even the most difficult job. At that moment, though, I was so angry, I felt as if I hated her, and I don't think I spoke to her for two weeks. But how wrong I was. It turned out to be the best move ever.

The summer after Year 11, just after you've finished your GCSEs, you tend to get a longer than usual break before school begins again in September. Normally, holidays zoom by in a flash, but this summer felt as if it was going on forever, because I knew that instead of returning to boring old school, I'd be off to Harrogate for my six-month Army training.

My family had a leaving party for me, which was actually a surprise. We were supposed to be celebrating grandad's birthday by having a barbecue round my auntie's house. I seem to remember him coming into the butcher's to buy the meat, and I may even have given him a little freebie as it was a special occasion. When it was closing time, I went home and had a shower and then made my way to my auntie's. I knocked on the front door, but there was no one there, so I went round the side and pushed through the back gate . . . Everyone—my friends, my whole family, my girlfriend at the time, some people from school—were standing there with a big Good Luck Harry! banner. I thought people would be sad that I was leaving, but they were all so happy for me, telling me I'll smash it, that I was the first one out of Slough and that they were so proud of me.

That was when my parents gave me my St Christopher sovereign coin on a chain. They'd had 'Our Hero, Harry' engraved onto the back, which made it really special. It was great to feel like they believed in my choice to go into the military. That day, I was also given a booklet, and everyone who was close to me had written something in it. One page had been left blank except for a quote from the Bible: 'What God has put together, Let no man take apart'. Later, that became my first ever tattoo, when I had it written on my right forearm. (I'd always wanted a tattoo but wasn't sure my mum was ever going to allow it. I think the only reason she let me get that first one was because it was about faith.) Since then, I've had a few tattoos, including a cross on my right hand, which was for her.

The best thing about the barbecue that day was that I felt as if I was going with the encouragement of the people I loved. But the reason the quote from the Bible meant so much to me—enough to get it inked on my body forever—was because I knew I wasn't going just by myself; I was going with the support of God, too. He'd shown me this path, and I was grateful to have the opportunity to get on and make my family proud.

When I began my Army training, I discovered that the people who were getting trades like me (Tradies, as we were called) were mixed up with the Infantry soldiers. However, whereas we were training for six months, the Infantry were training for a whole year. After that year, it was possible they could be deployed straight to Afghanistan, so they needed skills; they needed to be sure they knew what to do in battle.

The Infantry soldiers were the coolest bunch, and some of them were becoming paratroopers, so naturally I loved chatting to them and hearing about their training. At the same time, it only made me wish I was doing what they were.

Also, the Infantry looked down on the Tradies, assuming we just wanted to hide behind the front line, but that wasn't the case at all. I'd take every opportunity I could to prove that to them, including fighting and battering their man in the boxing ring.

Those first six weeks were really tough because they're designed to filter out the people who don't want to be there. They worked you hard physically; they shaved your head (sad, as I love my hair) to make sure you knew that the Army and the team came before you; they got you to you make your bed properly, and your clothes always had to be clean, pressed and folded properly, which some people found quite a chore after a full day of training. My mum always taught me to be clean and tidy, so I didn't struggle with that, but not everyone in my twelve-man dorm was the same. The tough thing was that if someone stank or didn't make their bed correctly, the whole room got done for it, and we might lose phone privileges or have to run extra laps. So, it was important (though not easy) to make sure that people were doing their hygiene. We learned how to subtly suggest to someone that they might like to use the vacuum cleaner when we'd finished, or that they might fancy a shower, given how much trouble they got into after not taking one the last time. Those early days in the Army taught me how to deal with people and persuade them to do what I wanted, which was definitely a skill I'd need later on in life.

Some people didn't make it through those demanding first six weeks, but I knew I wanted to be there from the second I arrived: I was having a blast. I got to run around and learn about what the Army did, and even though I was getting paid, it didn't feel like work at all. The only difficult thing was being away from my family. We got our phones for twenty minutes every night (sometimes not even that, if someone in my troop had done something stupid and lost us our privileges), and it was such a short amount of time in which to juggle speaking with all the people in my life. Normally, I'd just FaceTime my mum, because I missed her and knew she'd report back to everyone else.

What made being away from home harder was that my dog Sherman (named after the British World War Two tank) passed away during those first six weeks. That was the saddest thing ever because we were best friends. I knew it was a possibility he might die, and I even remember my dad telling me, 'Say goodbye to Sherman, might be the last time you see him', before I left, but I never believed that would be the case. I always asked my mum to show me Sherman, and then one night she just wouldn't.

That was probably the time I first learned to be strong and to put my emotions aside. I was in a dorm with eleven other boys, and I really couldn't be lying in my bed, sobbing about my dog. People in the Army are supposed to be made of steel, and we had a sixteen-mile run to do in the morning. No matter what I was feeling, I had to get the job done.

After six weeks, to celebrate getting through the First Phase of training, there's a Pass Out Parade. It was brilliant, as my whole family could come to watch me. I hadn't seen them in all that time, and it was great to be able to show them the effort I'd put in.

During those early days, as well as everything I was asked to do, I'd also take the group out for runs in the evening and practise my boxing. I was always making sure that not only my bed but others' were made properly (for obvious reasons), and if I was doing any exercises like burpees or press-ups wrong, I'd apologise and make sure it never happened again. The Army want you to pass the First Phase, so they do encourage you, but they also want to make sure that when you make a mistake, you learn from it and get better. I think trying and learning from your failures is what makes good soldiers. That's certainly what I took away from my time in the Army. Later, when I took part in *Celebrity SAS*, I struggled because this idea didn't seem to apply, which meant the experience felt nothing like the military to me. That would lead to one of the darkest moments in my life, but we'll get there later.

Following the Pass Out Parade, new roles are assigned, and they made me Platoon Sergeant. This meant I had to look after thirty-two other kids, making sure their rooms were perfect and their stuff was laid out ready for inspection the next day. It made me try even harder to coerce everyone into doing what the Army required of them.

If the first six weeks were about learning discipline, the second were when proper soldier training began. You got deployed into the field where you learnt to camp, live off the land, cook your rations, keep your rubbish properly and generally be out, either moving between positions or holding a position. Then you were taught about weapon handling, correct fire drills, tactics, navigation, etc.—everything you would need to survive by yourself or as part of a team if you were deployed in the field. Becoming proficient in actual life skills you could use out in the real world (but would never be taught in school) was hugely attractive to me.

While I was absorbing this basic soldiering, I also had to carry out my Platoon Sergeant duties, which meant making sure the teams I was looking after had supplies and rations, as well as learning things like how to make decisions in the field, what to do in case of medical emergencies and how to communicate properly on the radio if making a call was needed.

For a 16 or 17-year-old, this was a lot of work and a huge amount of pressure, but when I thought about what else I could be doing back in Slough, I felt good. Instead of being at home as usual, I'm out in the field, on a Wednesday, at 3 a.m., on a night reconnaissance, using night-vision goggles to get information on an enemy vehicle, before going in to attack at dawn. That had to be better than dragging myself out of bed late to go to a class I couldn't be bothered with.

The truth is that I loved those early days. It was fun, I was doing well, I was fitter than I've ever been, and it felt like I was doing something with my life and moving forward. Sometimes, I honestly wish I could go back there. I was so happy.

But Phase Two was coming, and everything was about to change.

8

THE ARMY: THE MIDDLE YEARS

PHASE TWO OF MY ARMY career changed me.

Now that I was training to become an aircraft technician, I was moved to Swindon and given my own room. In these new surroundings, I found myself in the company of guys who were in their late twenties or early thirties, who had been in the Army for over a decade and were just now deciding to transfer over to learn a trade. And, believe me, they weren't impressed that I was a Platoon Sergeant—they thought I was just a teacher's pet. I felt like a boy in a man's world.

Everything I'd built up in Harrogate seemed to mean nothing, and I really missed my life there. I used to run around, go to the gym and use my hands all day. Now it was back to books for much of the time. And when you're being marked on how much studying you've done and assessed by the grades you get in exams—rather than on your speed or strength—you start to get kind of lazy on fitness. If my legs were killing me from the previous day's training, or if I just couldn't be arsed, all I had to do was say I was going to the med centre (or offer some other flimsy excuse), and instead of doing PT, I could sit in my room and play *Call of Duty*.

That's when I began to lose a sense of what I enjoyed about the Army. It was also about the time I started to drink too much.

As I said, some of the men alongside me on my training were transferees who'd come over from the Infantry. Many had been deployed to Afghanistan or Iraq or both, and I felt like a baby compared to them. That was hard because these guys were my idols. They'd seen so much action, and because of this, they were made of total steel. Naturally, when they asked if I was coming to the pub, I went.

Hearing their stories of dangerous missions and heroic action, I constantly felt surprised that we were even in the same room. I wanted to do what these guys had done. Yet, a lot of them weren't happy that they had worked hard for over a decade and were still only Privates. The lad living in the room opposite mine was twenty-six, had a family back home and now needed to get a trade to be able to support them. He'd done eleven years in the Infantry and was at the same level as I was.

Considering the courage these soldiers had shown, I thought they should be placed on a pedestal, and I told them so numerous times. I felt disappointed and a little angry on their behalf. They'd given everything for their country; they'd been in war zones getting shot at, putting their lives on the line; they knew many soldiers who'd been injured, suffered severe PTSD or died. And then the second they got home, they'd have to start worrying about their overdraft. That was when I realised how right my mum had been about this being a good path for my life. It allowed me to advance further, make more money and have better prospects in general—important, as I wanted to be able to provide for my family when I had one.

Listening to their stories, I felt I wanted to help carry these soldiers' burdens in whatever way I could. I'm a proud ambassador for the military and was delighted to be invited to present VE Day 80 at the Royal Albert Hall in July 2025. But if anyone ever asks me what it's like to be a veteran, I'll correct them and say I never class myself that way because I haven't actually seen conflict.

Whatever has happened in my life, I'm glad I've never had to worry about coming back to my family in one piece. Mum was wise about that aspect too.

I may have had very different life experiences from some of my fellow trainees, but I've always been good at surviving in a group. I think everyone generally adapts to whatever environment they're in, and my family would say you could stick me in any room and I'll be chatting to everyone by the end of the night. That came to be one of my most useful skills when I was on *The Traitors*, but while I had some natural talent before I left home, my ability to speak to all kinds of people was honed in the Army.

Given that I wanted to be friends with the people I regarded as heroes, I took every opportunity I could to go and chat with them. I'm not sure any man, particularly a British one, opens up about anything too deep without a few beers in him, so typically (as I mentioned) we'd go to the pub where I'd get to hear about their unbelievable lives and what it was like going to places where war was actually happening. That was so cool. More difficult was finding out how serving in the Army had affected them and the issues they were dealing with.

I think a willingness to speak about this stuff is the major difference between the older generations of veterans who fought in the Second World War and today's soldiers.

Whereas our grandparents, and even our parents, might never say a word about what they'd seen and just get on with life, now there's encouragement to talk about your mental health and to share tough experiences. And as I didn't have any heavy baggage of my own and wouldn't respond with my own challenges, a lot of the lads confided in me.

This was when I started to realise how good I was at compartmentalising. I could hear people's problems and stories, put them in a box and not think about them. I believe this was another reason people spoke to me; they knew that whatever they told me was locked away and would never come up again. Sometimes I felt like a therapist for some of the guys, as they offloaded their problems onto me and I absorbed them.

I love being a safe space for people, and I'm always happy to be regarded as such by my family and friends. But, given that I never offload back, some worry about how I process my own difficult thoughts and feelings. My answer is simple: prayer. When I'm dealing with my own problems, all I need to do is lock into my faith, sit down and pray. Talking to God gives me the same sensation as sharing difficulties with a trusted friend: it lifts a weight off my shoulders, because I know that God has whatever is troubling me now, and I don't need to worry about it anymore.

I think the push for people to be more open about their emotions and to air whatever they're going through can only be a good thing. I always recommend people find their own safe space to offload. I talk about my problems with God; other people choose a licensed therapist. I encourage you to find whatever works for you, open up and trust in the world.

Later on, the person I'd have to remind to do this was myself.

This second period of learning was a tough eighteen months. After leaving school because I hated books and didn't feel I could really learn that way, I was back in the classroom.

At first, we focused on the basics of maths, physics and other subjects. I might learn nothing but the foundations of maths for six full weeks, and even though I then had an exam to sit, I felt as if things were going in one ear and out the other. You need to get 60% for a pass, and I did somehow manage that with the foundation subjects. But then came really difficult things like the Theory of Flight, and there was a module on Aircraft Logs, where you literally go through massive books of minor details and learn how to make your own logs. It's all electronic now, so everything's a lot easier to do, but at the time, I had to get out these huge tomes and sit and pick out tiny details from masses of information. As I'm dyslexic, this felt like banging my head against the desk. I'd be counting down the days until we finished some of those modules.

Not only did I find the work hard, I also couldn't see the practical application (how would learning this stuff help me fix a helicopter?), and the result was that I twice failed my exams and had to go back and do the course again. Each time, I thought about leaving, and even though I was convinced by then that getting a trade was a smart move, I'd constantly be asking myself why I didn't just chuck it all in and become a paratrooper.

Mum knew I didn't think the course was working for me, but she kept reminding me that when I was doing my

GCSEs, and really put my head down, I eventually passed my exams. She encouraged me that once I'd passed, I could leave the subject and never think about it ever again. Actually, that didn't apply to Avionics! I realised I would need most of what I was being taught, but it helped to be reassured that I could pass something I was finding difficult that didn't involve learning with my hands.

Amidst the struggle with my studies, I was still using my hands for something. In the Army, any company with men who boxed would compete at regular boxing nights. As my entire company consisted of aircraft technicians, no one seemed to expect us to be any good: normally, we'd be maintaining aircraft in a base somewhere far from the action on the front line, and I think they thought we just sat there, drinking tea with our feet up. Meanwhile, people like the Infantry did the nitty gritty work of going on patrol, getting shot at by the Taliban and all that. The Army is a hierarchy, and the closer you are to danger, the nearer you are to the top. So, if someone's job is more dangerous than yours, they tend to look down on you and assume you're weaker than them.

Throughout my life, I've felt as if I have a point to prove about being smart enough and tough enough. Boxing gave me a chance to prove I was the latter at least, so whenever I was up against a soldier from another company, I'd give it everything. And pretty much every time, I'd win.

Nonetheless, the feeling that I was missing out on the paratrooper life I craved kept coming back, and the turmoil of wondering if I should be doing something else kept me miserable for months. Luckily, one of the people I boxed with was my section commander, who had been in the

Army for ten years and was always great to talk to. When I eventually told her I might still transfer back to the Infantry, she warned against it. Why, she asked, did I think so many from the Infantry were transferring here to get a trade? She told me that I was already three steps ahead of everyone else. While I wanted to leave off learning from aircraft log books to run around a field shooting things, she saw the future. She knew that if you became a paratrooper but then got injured or busted your knee or were medically discharged for any reason, the best job you could pick up would be as a bouncer at a nightclub or in the security sector. Whereas, if I got a trade, the moment I left the Army, I could get a well-paid position at an airport or on the trains. That got through to me, as I wanted to make money to better the lives of those around me. The turmoil went away, and I really started to feel better.

It also helped that my studies were becoming more practical. I was doing things like wiring and welding, and having physical sight of the electronics it was my job to fix. Being hands-on again, I sailed through the next few months of my studies, performing so well that I was promoted to Lance Corporal. Numerous people reminded me that it can take ten years to become a Lance Corporal if you're a paratrooper (just in case I was still torn about continuing as a Tradie). That may sound unfair, but what people serving in the Infantry don't always understand is that there's a level of responsibility that comes with signing off on an aircraft. Being only eighteen or nineteen at the time, it felt as if I was being given a crazy amount of responsibility, but I was still in training for another two months, so I didn't have to worry too much for now.

I was becoming an adult and maturing quickly. But the truth is that in training, life feels a bit artificial because making mistakes can be regarded as part of the learning process. It's only when you join a battalion that the real world hits you. Whereas practising on an aircraft and getting something wrong means it's likely to break down, being part of a battalion and getting something wrong means a plane or helicopter might crash out of the sky and kill people. It really could be life or death.

When I joined the battalion, I had to start getting to know new people again. As we were all having to cope with the kind of pressure I've just described, we appreciated how important it was to trust others, and that helped us connect. By this point, I was understandably keen to settle into more long-term friendships.

Admittedly, I already knew one guy in my battalion. And I hated him. His name was Joshua Arneson, and the first time we met, I wanted to beat him up. We had bumped into each other during my Phase Two, when he was training to become an aircraft technician. Aircraft technicians are responsible for putting the engine into an aircraft and installing new computers, while avionics technicians (like me) basically go in and wire the whole thing and make it fly. So, our jobs went hand-in-hand, and I think that's why someone introduced us in a pub. Because Josh doesn't like beer (which is mental), he'd had about twenty Jäger Bombs by this point. He asked me where I was from, and I said, 'I'm from Slough', and he was like, 'Cool, you must be thick then.' I switched and wanted to punch him. Fortunately, someone led me away, but my first impression was that I really detested him.

The next time I saw Josh was when we were in battalion together, and, surprise, surprise, we got on like a house on fire. He's now one of my closest friends, and definitely the best one I made in the Army. His room was opposite mine, and we'd laugh about that first night, and argue about who'd beat who up. We were deployed together multiple times over the course of a year, and as I said, the pressure of the job brought us together. (He's since apologised for the 'thick' comment!)

One of the great things about being in the Army is that you get to meet people from all walks of life. One night, I was hanging out with a load of Fijians, learning a game called Tucky. Tucky's pretty simple: you pour the alcohol you have into one bottle, then sit in a circle with your legs crossed, singing 'Red Red Wine' by UB40 (the Fijians seemed to love that), passing the bottle around until it's empty. In situations like this, I'd always be thinking to myself, how could a kid from Slough ever have met these people if I hadn't joined the Army?

Similarly, there were a few Gurkhas in my battalion, and I idolised these guys. You hear stories about the Gurkhas the whole time when you're in the Army, because they're such an elite force. I think even to join up in Nepal, they have to run up a mountain with about 50 kilos of stones in their bag. Being in the British Army is their dream, so when they get here, they work really hard. There was a Gurkha sniper who'd done about fifteen years in the Infantry on my avionics course. I got to chat to him, and I remember thinking how bizarre it was that this guy, who was the best of the best at what he did, was now learning the Theory of Flight with me—and that's on top of the challenge of English not being his first language.

These guys were so good. I remember one time when I first got into the battalion, we were walking around on patrol in the mountains at three in the morning. We've come to a bush, and someone thinks they've heard something, so we've gone into a formation and taken a knee at the ridge line. But the second we stop, we hear nothing. Until suddenly someone over our shoulder asks softly what we're looking for. We all jump. A whole patrol of Gurkhas has somehow managed to sneak right up on us, within whispering distance. We were all like, How did you manage that? I thought they'd just been careful not to step on sticks and stones, but they showed us . . . they take their boots and socks off to muffle any sound. When they go out on patrol, they're walking around barefoot, feeling everything they're stepping on. Nuts.

Our battalion was quite small, so I really got to know these guys, and I have nothing but respect for every single one of them.

When you're in a battalion, depending on the type of aircraft you're working on, you can basically choose where you're deployed, as certain aircraft only go out to certain places. You can also choose your UK base. I got really lucky. Salisbury was only an hour away from Slough, which meant I could go home every weekend. I would be Corporal Clark from Monday to Friday, but then I could just be Harry on the weekends. Most people didn't have any family nearby, so they literally lived on camp. And really, the only form of recreation there was going to the Army bar, so they'd get smashed all weekend, every weekend.

If you let the Army consume your life, it can get quite lonely, because you're not putting time and energy into the relationships you have with people outside. Being able to go home to my family every weekend was something I thanked God for, because it meant that if I was having a terrible week and missed everyone, it would only be a few days before I could see them all again.

Life in the Army can give you the highest of highs. Going on those night patrols, getting to see the Gurkhas in action, watching helicopters I'd fixed come back from missions without a single thing wrong with them (and feeling reassured I'd done my job brilliantly)—I'm so grateful to have had those experiences and wouldn't trade them for the world.

But everyone has lows, and my lowest point was about to come.

9

THE DARK DAYS

WHEN I FIRST GOT to the battalion, I loved it. I was learning the job; we had a routine (sports on a Wednesday, the bar after work), and the whole thing was just great. Then I was deployed to a place where the weather was incredible. We could end the day by going cliff-jumping or snorkelling, and I used to say to myself, 'Can't do this in the UK!'

I was out there when I finished my training and was given my blue beret. There was supposed to be a ceremony back home, but Covid messed with the timings, so the whole thing was done over a live stream. Seeing the faces of my family and then being able to go to a beach bar with my mates and celebrate in style wasn't terrible. On 13th April 2021, I got my wings, and that will always be one of the proudest moments of my life.

I loved being out on deployment. It felt so good in the sun that I almost never wanted to leave, but the truth was that I was running away from home. Me and my girlfriend at the time were having issues, and rather than dealing with them, I made sure I was out of the country as much as possible. One year, I think I did nine months straight with just one two-week window in between. Many of the other people in my battalion had partners or families back home, and to avoid missing an anniversary or their son or daughter's birthday, they'd often be looking for a volunteer (who was doing the same job) to be deployed instead of them. That's when I would step up and offer to take their place. Also, if you were good and there was a sergeant who wanted you in their team, they'd ask you to go along as part of their crew, and I'd take up these offers too. There really is no better feeling in the world than fixing an aircraft, watching it fly away and then seeing it come back later with no problems. You'd know you'd done good.

Over time, I built up a lot of leave. I thought I was just fine—I was focusing on my job, going for beers and enjoying being surrounded by people constantly. But underneath the surface, things were beginning to take quite a toll. As I mentioned, the Army can be a lonely place. You get to know who you're working with, but not as well as your friends and family. Even though I was making some great connections, nothing ever substitutes for what you get from the people who really care for you. I realise now that I was putting a lot of distance between myself and those I love.

All of us in camp probably felt a little homesick at times, and one unfortunate side effect of that kind of loneliness is a sadness that can be hard to shake. I lost some friends along the way due to mental health reasons. Some were really close, some less so, but whenever anyone dies by suicide, it hits you that you're in the same position as them, in the same place in your life. You might have been having a drink with them only the other day and remember them talking about the people in their lives they were excited to see again, the future they had planned, and how they were looking forward to this or that next week, or when they got back to the UK. Now they'd never do those things. That brought home to me how alone we sometimes are and, because you can very rarely see these things coming, how much chaos there is in the universe.

I'd always believed that God was with me, but I began to feel lost because I couldn't understand how this could happen to people. And rather than praying, I'd go to the pub with my mates to try to work things out. At first, you'd be toasting the person who had died with a beer, which you knew they'd love, but then you'd drink just to make yourself feel better. And that would only work temporarily, because the next day, the hangover would mean you were in a worse place to deal with difficult emotions.

Then, while I was still away on deployment, my ex and I broke up. We'd been together for seven years, since I was in my early years at secondary school, so I literally knew nothing else but being with her. She was my first love and the person I thought I was going to stay with forever. It hit me hard.

I believe a break-up is never one person's fault. There are two sides to every story, and both people contribute to it in their own way. I'm not going to go into the gory details here. Let's just say that each of us did things we weren't proud of, particularly towards the end. By that stage, we were almost unrecognisable from the couple we'd been before, and I could barely remember what I loved about our relationship. But when it fell apart, I still missed it.

I was far away from my family and the people I cared about, but at the same time, the UK felt as if it wasn't the safe space I needed to be. It was filled with memories of my ex, and she was still around in the area I grew up in, so there was a chance I might see her. I just wasn't in the right place for that. My only answer was to drink and smoke, and basically to turn into a pig. I went out boozing every night, which would ruin the next day, and I wouldn't do any fitness whatsoever. I still loved working, but I couldn't really be bothered any more, probably because I was hungover. I thought I was getting away with things and hoped that no one had noticed. Then my Staff Sergeant called me into their office and told me I needed to go home and sort myself out.

I was sad, fat, lonely and being sent away from the work I enjoyed, which was a large part of my identity at the time, to somewhere I didn't want to be. It felt like my whole life had fallen apart. And I was about to get punched while I was down.

When I arrived home in October, I was in a terrible state mentally. And shortly afterwards, something happened that would send me into a really dark place.

One night, I went to a family party in Windsor at one of our favourite bars. I'd had a couple of drinks, but I wasn't having the best time, so when it turned out that someone needed to go and get George, who seemed to be lost, I took the excuse to leave temporarily (and have a cigarette). A few mates came with me: my best friend Brown, along with my close friend Connor and my cousin Henry. We were walking past the arches in Windsor, me on the phone to my brother, when all of a sudden, we were jumped from behind. I was hit really hard over the back of the head with something and went straight down onto the cold pavement.

I can't remember a lot after that because I was floating in and out of consciousness, but I do recall getting up to go over to Brown, who looked in a really bad way. The image of him lying there bleeding still haunts me. My next memory

1

2

1 George and Harry, 2006

2 Delilah, Harry, George (holding baby Matilda) and Alf, 2008

3

4

3 The Clark Family, 2011

4 Harry, Alf and George, 2010

6 

7 

5 Harry boxing, 2015
6 Harry and Grandad Dave, 2018
Harry winning boxing award, 2022

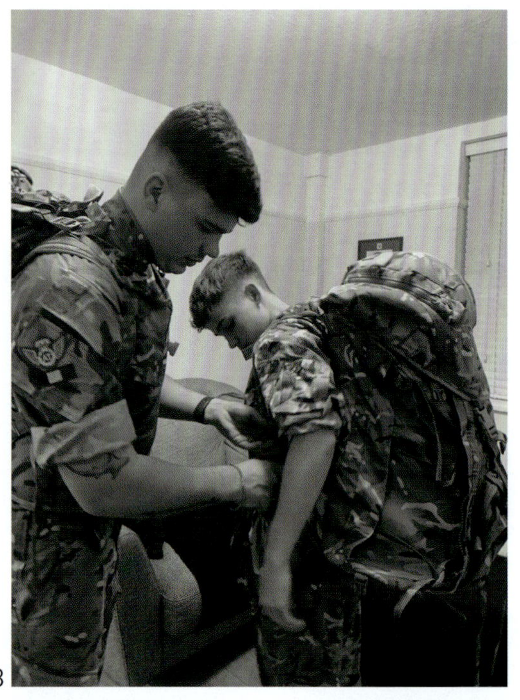

8

9

10

8 Harry and Alf in the Army, 2022 9 Harry with Granny, 2023
10 Nana and Harry, 2022

11

12

11 Alf, Matilda, George, Harry and Delilah, 2022
12 Alf, Mum and Harry, 2025

13

14

13 Harry and Paul "The Traitors: Live Experience", 2023
14 Harry and Anna at the BAFTAs, 2024

15

16

15 Jaz, Harry and Diane Carson at the National Television Awards 2024
16 Harry at the BAFTAs, 2025

17

18

19

20

17-20 Harry, 2025

is of being in the ambulance and being really confused about why they'd written all these numbers down my arm in white marker pen. I remember getting to the hospital and asking one of the paramedics if they had a cigarette, because I hadn't had a chance to have one earlier. I was clearly in shock, acting as if nothing major had happened, thinking we'd only got punched once (and that had happened to me thousands of times in the ring), and assuming we were all fine. We just needed to dust ourselves off. Then we could get an Uber to pick up my brother and go back to the party. It wasn't until we walked into A&E, where Mum, Dad and George were waiting, and I saw the look on their faces, that I realised how bad things really were.

We think the guys who jumped us mistook us for someone else, but whoever they were, they meant business. As well as bashing me on the head, they'd tried to cut my ear off with something and, whether it was from the first hit or other blows they'd got in, they'd knocked my front teeth out, fractured my orbital socket (the area of bone around your eye) and given me a bleed on the brain. If I wasn't aware I was in a bad way when I arrived, it became clear to me when my mates were quickly discharged from hospital and I stayed in. Luckily, I didn't have to have surgery, but the place in my mouth where my teeth were missing became infected, and I got an abscess, which kept me in longer.

And what affected me more than anything was that the person I most wanted to be there by my side didn't turn up. Days and days went by, and they never showed.

Sitting in that hospital bed alone one night, something in me broke. A wall went up: a wall against people; a wall against the world; a wall against anything good in my life.

I hadn't lost all faith, but I was in such a dark place that I began questioning it. I was someone who had devoted their life to God. I'd prayed every day, gone to church, contributed so much to those Bible classes, and here I was, in the worst place and at the hardest point in my life. I couldn't help but ask why.

Totally miserable, I felt as if I was dragging down those around me.

I began to think that maybe they would be better off if I just wasn't there.

For months, over what was one of the worst Christmases ever, I kept asking myself why I was being put through this. And that was when the feeling of loneliness came back in a big way. I was never great at talking about my emotions (and I certainly wasn't going to tell my mum and dad, especially at Christmas, that I was thinking about ending it all), but I could normally talk to my dad about things and know he'd listen. Now I couldn't even tell him I was struggling.

There was a lot of love around me, yet I almost couldn't feel it, I think because I knew I had to get myself out of this. There was shame, too, that I'd dug such a hole in the first place. I remembered being this ripped, confident guy; now I was touching 100 kilos and seriously overweight, and all I could think was, I've done this to myself. When you're suffering that badly, you tend to block out everything else, and I'm not sure anyone can say anything or do anything to help you.

The only thing that was getting through to me was music. I've always loved listening to music, and one of the ways my mum says my dad and I are really similar is that we come home from the pub, sit in the corner and put our favourite tracks on really loudly, no matter what time it is or how many people are trying to sleep. I now have a Mac Miller tattoo, as his music means a lot to me and I want to honour the man.

Mum was still trying desperately to help (I can't imagine how upset my parents must have been seeing me so low), and I remember one day she said, 'Why don't you start praying again?' Given how I was feeling, I thought this was a terrible idea and really didn't want to, but I was out of other options. Nothing else seemed to be working, so I'd maybe try it and see . . . When I sat down to pray that first night, I wasn't praying for a full recovery. I prayed God would let me see my little sister's birthday, which was in January. I didn't need a sign, and I didn't want God to get me there; I knew I needed to do that for myself. I just asked him to give me the strength to see tomorrow . . . tomorrow might be a better day.

When I was a kid, I prayed for things I wanted: a bike, to get really good at the violin, or for Chelsea to win the league. Now, that shifted. I no longer wanted things I didn't have; I wanted to be able to appreciate the things I did. I thanked God for my family; I thanked him for music, I thanked him for all the things that brought me joy, and I thanked him for allowing me to be here for one more day. What you don't immediately realise when you're doing this is that you're also inadvertently reminding yourself of all the good you have in your life. I started to realise that I didn't care if there was or wasn't a God; all that mattered was that I had these great things. And that gave me a reason to keep going.

It didn't happen overnight, but I started to get better. I made it to my little sister's birthday and then gave myself more things to look forward to. I was asked if I wanted to box in the Royal Artillery Championships, a week-long competition against the best in the military. If I wanted to stand a chance, I knew I had to give it 110%, so I abandoned the drinking and smoking instantly. From January to March, I went to four or five sessions every day, like it was my job, and I ate chicken and rice daily too. I began to lose weight and gain muscle. I felt like my old self again. I was gearing up for the championships and was so excited about it. I had the fight back in me.

Looking back now, I see this terrible time in my life less as a curse and more as a test of my faith. I'm not saying that God sent me into the dark place; I believe more that those dark days happened, and my faith in the world and that things would work out allowed me to come out the other side. I'd always thought I appreciated what I had, but now I knew for certain that there were good things in my life. And even better, I believed that there were great things in my future.

And that was exactly when I met Anna.

10
ANNA

FALLING IN LOVE WITH ANNA was the easiest thing in the world. How we met is a romantic story, and it begins, like all the most romantic stories ever, in PRYZM nightclub in Brighton.

I'd never made a trip to Brighton before. I don't know why I would. It's a busy place, it's expensive, and it's quite hard to get to from Slough, unless you drive. However, one day in March, as I was preparing for the RA Championships, my cousin told me that he had a fight in a place on the seafront. And though he'd never seemed to care much before if I saw him box, for some reason, he was really insisting I come to this match.

It was two weeks before the Championships, and I wasn't drinking, so I think he just wanted me to give him a lift. That meant he and my mates could go clubbing and get a ride back after. I wasn't sure, but on the other hand, I did fancy a night out. All we ever did was go out in Windsor, so even if Brighton was a long way, at least it was a change. Fresh club, fresh scene, fresh birds.

That day, we got in the car—me, my two best mates and my little brother—to see my cousin box. There were loads of other members of the family there too, so we all watched the fight together. Afterwards, Alf the Great got a lift home with someone else, and me and the boys went out.

We had no idea where we were going. But then we spotted PRYZM on the seafront. It's quite hard to miss as it's the biggest nightclub you've ever seen—a huge building with three massive floors. We went in, and after a few minutes I was thinking I needed to go to the toilet, so I leaned over to one of my mates and said, 'Hey, I need a wee', and he was like, 'All right, let's try and find one.' So up we all go to the top floor, and I'm looking around, and then I see her, buying vapes with her mates at this little kiosk thing . . . and looking at me. People ask what initially attracted me to Anna, and it's pretty simple, really: she's fit. I was a single guy, and the minute I saw her, I thought, she's absolutely beautiful. That place felt like the pit of hell—so dark, so busy, so sweaty—and here was an angel in the middle of it.

Anna may not agree with this story, but she was giving me the eye. I promise you, I would never approach someone without encouragement, and Anna was looking at me in a way that said she wanted to marry me and have my kids. Just to check I wasn't imagining it, I turned away and back again, and she was still giving me the eye. I knew she wanted me to say something, but I needed to be sure, so I said to my mates, 'Hold up, boys, do me a favour. Let's walk past this group of girls, and if I turn around and she's still looking at me, I'll go over.' We walk past the group, and when I look back, yes, she's still looking at me, so I was like, right, here we go . . .

I walked across and gave her my best line: 'Excuse me, darling, do you know where the toilets are?' She gave me a different look then. More, no one's ever approached me like that before. I couldn't tell if she was impressed or not. But as she's from Brighton and this wasn't her first night in PRYZM, she was the right person to ask. She told me there was a toilet on every floor, looking at me almost in disbelief that I hadn't noticed the others I'd passed. It was a bit of a cold shoulder, a bit of hard to get, but I love that. I apologised and said I wasn't local, and we talked about where we were from. We asked each other what we did. She said she was a singer and posted stuff online, and I was like, 'Cool'; I told her I was in the Army, and got 'That's a red flag', because she had a friend who had been with someone in the Army. I asked her if she thought I looked like a red flag, and she said she wasn't sure yet.

I thought we were getting on really, really well, proper bouncing off each other, but the boys were calling me over, and I still needed to pee, so I told her I had to go. I asked if I could have her number, in case I got lost again, and she must have thought we were getting on, too, because she gave it to me. Then I walked off.

When I came out of the loo, my mates dragged me to the worst room in the place, which was only playing pop/chart music. We're more into rap and hip-hop, so after a few minutes, we changed to the R&B room. And who was in the middle of the dance floor? Anna. She pointed at me, and I went right over.

At the end of the night, I offered to take her and her mate home before I drove to Slough, as long as we could all stop off at a McDonald's on the way. It wasn't chicken and rice, but I was starving. So technically, our first meal together was a Big Mac Meal (Anna) and Chicken Nuggets and Chips (for me, obviously).

I thought about her in the car all the way back. We may have met in a massive, sweaty nightclub with sticky floors and finished up in a Maccy D's, but it was still one of the most romantic nights ever. I hadn't been planning on meeting anyone, but I had met her. And I was hooked.

Anna told me later that she wasn't looking for anything serious that night either. She didn't want a boyfriend at the time, and I had obviously just broken up with my ex, so I wasn't looking for a girlfriend. That meant things were chilled, right from the start.

But though there was no pressure, we texted every single day. I'd actually already broken the seal of texting, because I sent her a message when I was in PRYZM that didn't come through to her until she got home that night (or that morning), so there it was when she woke up. It just said, 'This is Harry, the boy from the Army', with a purple devil emoji. No chance of me playing it cool, then, but I didn't mind. I loved messaging back and forth with Anna.

We continued all through Sunday, but that evening I had to go back to my Army camp for boxing. We FaceTimed on Monday and were planning to meet up on the weekend, but then I had a little stroke of luck. In sparring on Tuesday, I got a cut under my eye, which meant I couldn't carry on and was sent home. On Wednesday evening, we had our first date (technically, it was a double date, as we both brought friends along, but it still counts), and the rest is history. During the week, we would be apart, but we'd go to each other's houses on the weekend and FaceTime every night. She met my family, and I met hers. We became boyfriend and girlfriend: she said she loved me, and I said I loved her too. To cut a long story short, we had a great first year together.

Having brought myself out of my darkest moment ever, I felt as if Anna was my reward. I was fitter, stronger and more committed to my faith than ever before, and now I'd been given someone who fitted me perfectly. We met dancing in a club to songs we both like; we had fun, and our relationship has continued to be fun because we both value that so much. Anna's big on family, and she was already thinking about working for the future of the one she wanted to have, so we're very similar in that.

But we're opposites, too. Whereas I'm always shooting for the stars and thinking really big (I want ten children, but also enough money to make a good life for them), Anna's more connected with reality. If we go on holiday, she'll worry about what will happen if we're delayed; if we go on a motorway, she'll worry about accidents, and if the traffic slows to a stop, she'll lock the doors, just in case . . . Despite all these things, I know she feels safe with me. She always says my love language is acts of service, and if one of those can be to make her feel protected while she's with me, then I'm happy.

I feel safe with her, too. I've never been a great sleeper; often, I'm just lying there, looking up at the ceiling, thinking . . . And if I do want to get off to sleep, I've got to put something calming on the TV, like a nature documentary, or listen to some natural sounds on Spotify. Functioning well on limited sleep was a really useful skill in the Army because you could never be sure how much you'd get, where you'd be sleeping (it could be outside in the rain next to your rifle), or if you'd need to be up and ready at any minute. Plus, you might have to share a room with some loud snorers. But with Anna, a lot of the time we FaceTimed, we'd fall asleep together while still on the phone. And now, lying next to her or with my head on her chest, I find I can sleep like a baby.

Despite us having such similar ideas about the family we want to create, Anna's family life is completely different to mine. There are always loads of people (being loud) in our house. She comes from a smaller family, and at quite a young age, her brothers moved out, so when she was twelve, she felt almost like an only child. Also, while the closest my family got to fame was Peter Osgood, her brothers have been in the public eye in a big way. I think if you grow up with public recognition, you have to reach a certain level of maturity quite quickly, and Anna has done that.

However, having watched her brothers and having developed her own public profile, she's not only seen the best the entertainment industry can offer, but also the worst, and this makes her quite cautious. Because I have no fear—I'm a risk-taker—sometimes when Anna strongly advised me against something, I'd have no idea why. (After the last couple of years, I understand better.)

The darker side of fame and social media hit us about a year after we got together. Things had been amazing up till then. As I was still in the Army, we had our own lives, which I think is important in a relationship, but we'd spend as much time as possible together. Anna appreciated that I loved the Army, and I was beginning to understand her job a little bit, so I got that she'd sometimes go on these big trips away where everything was paid for . . . And then, one day, when I'd got up early to go to the gym, thousands of messages suddenly came through to my phone. She finds this hard to talk about even now, but essentially, another influencer on their trip away had said that Anna had cheated on me.

Of course, she hadn't. But as the papers and social media ran with the story, many assumed it must be true, and most of the messages I was receiving were people hating on her. This was my first taste of fame, and I wasn't sure what to do with it. Anna and I had built up trust over the previous twelve months, and I trusted her still, but it wasn't easy. That's when I realised we might need to start trying to work out how to keep our lives private.

In our second year together, after glimpsing some negative aspects of Anna's career, it occurred to me that I wasn't particularly enjoying mine either. The Army is great if you don't have someone to miss. (Obviously, I missed my family all the time, but maybe I was used to that.) Now, I had a girlfriend I was really excited about, I wanted us to spend as much time together as possible, and I'd be counting down the days until Friday when I could drive to see her, in Slough or Brighton.

We'd had a tricky time, but now we were in a great place and, as Anna and I loved to go out together, we found ourselves in London a lot. I know I sound such a tourist, but I love London. I started to imagine working there, so that I could be close to Anna and we could spend the evenings together. Anna didn't work nine-to-five; her schedule was flexible, and I already had my trade and could get loads of different jobs, on the trains or with an airline.

Just as I was thinking about getting out of the Army, one of my officers called me. 'Clarky,' he said, 'I've got an opening spot. You can promote early. Do you want to be a Corporal?' I was honest and told him I wasn't sure what I was doing with my life, but he said I could sit the exams, get the qualifications and then if I wanted to leave, I would be in a position to ask for more money when I was offered my next job. I appreciated his advice and took it, even though it meant going back to Swindon to do the supervisor training to become a Corporal. The worst bit was that I was back in the classroom again, going over massive books of aircraft logs.

One day, distracted from work, missing Anna and idly checking my phone, a message popped up. 'Hi Harry, I'm a caster from X. We're casting for a new show called *The Traitors . . .*'

Obviously, the first thing I said was, 'I'm pretty sure this is a scam.' She assured me she was a real person, but that is what any scammer would say, so I left it for a bit. I needed to finish my course anyway.

It was only when I showed Anna the message that she said she thought it might be genuine, given that the person had left their email and phone number. We did look her up, and she wasn't a scammer (or else a really good one), and that was when I started to take the offer more seriously. I didn't need to be on TV, and after everything that had happened the year before, I wasn't sure I wanted to be famous. But I spent that night not sleeping, just staring at the ceiling. I felt as if I needed something different; I felt I needed a change. So, the next day after work, I called the number.

As I'd never seen *The Traitors*, the caster had to work hard to explain it to me, and she even told me everything that had happened in season 1. We had a long, long chat and then right at the end, she said, 'Oh, and you can win up to £120,000.' I was like, 'Why didn't you start with that? I'm in!' I knew I had accumulated enough leave to take time out for the show without having to quit the Army, and I did think—because *The Traitors* was about lying and the Army was about trust—that they wouldn't grant me permission, so I'd have to take private leave (like holiday allowance from work) anyway. I was still planning to get a job on the trains, and I'd already spoken to someone who'd offered me one, but it seemed this was an opportunity I couldn't pass up.

Anna admits she was cautious. She hadn't watched season 1 of the show either and didn't know what being on it involved. Also, she hadn't signed up to have a famous boyfriend. (Our accounts were private, so the only way the casters could have seen me was on someone else's social media.) But I was thinking about the money and how great it would be to win it, give some to my family and have some left for a deposit on a house for our own family in the future. Cautious as she was, I loved this woman and wanted to provide for her, and this was my chance to do exactly that.

Yet, as Anna pointed out, we were a long way from anything happening. Forty thousand people had applied to be on the show, and I was one of 200 they were interviewing on Zoom.

That's why we were both so surprised when, in the middle of the summer of 2023, the producers called me and told me that they needed me on a train to Inverness the following week.

As scary and unknown as this next chapter of my life was going to be, I was armed with the love and support of the girl who took my breath away that night in Brighton. With Anna beside me, I knew I could take on the world.

11
THE TRAITORS: PART I

SO THERE I WAS, standing at King's Cross Station, waiting to get on a train to Inverness. It was the end of August, but it was definitely not warm. Despite wearing jeans and a thick blue hoodie, I was still shaking a bit, but that wasn't just the cold: I was terrified. I was all by myself, with a one-way ticket in my hand, and everything I could need for potentially four weeks in a massive suitcase by my side . . . and I was going to appear on a BBC reality TV show. I still couldn't believe it.

On the long journey north, I thought back to the interviews I'd had with the producers just a couple of weeks before. In fact, they seemed more like relaxed chats. I guess they wanted to get a sense of me and what I might bring to a group dynamic. We never talked about the show itself, which was a relief because I hadn't seen the first season and was worried they were going to grill me about it. What I did know was that you could either be a Faithful or a Traitor, and when they asked me at the end of our chat if I had anything to add, I looked them in the eye and said, 'Please don't send me up there if I'm not going to be a Traitor.'

The main reason for this was that I knew I had the perfect cover story. I was in the military, and the Army is an organisation built on trust and loyalty. I was proud to be a part of it and had never strayed from my dedication to being a responsible member of a team. Being a Traitor was a great way to be a little bit naughty and get away with it. No one was going to believe I could go in there and lie to everyone. But I love to prove people wrong.

In any case, this was a game, and ultimately, I wasn't playing it to get to know a bunch of strangers; I was playing it to better the lives of my family and friends, who had known and loved me for twenty-two years. With the prize, I could pay off any debts, take my family on a proper holiday, and go out with everyone for dinner and not worry about the bill (which, when you're from such a big family, never happens). I didn't want to be on TV; I wanted to win, and I knew being a Traitor would give me the best chance.

I think some people worry about being cast as a Traitor because they're afraid they won't be able to keep it together, or they're concerned that playing such a role will feel like a betrayal of who they really are as a person. But as I sat on the train, that wasn't what was worrying me. I was preoccupied with the fact that as soon as we arrived at Inverness, they were going to take my phone off me. I've never been big into social media and actually gave up my phone for Lent one year, which turned out to be the easiest thing in the world. What I was really going to miss was looking up the Chelsea scores (though actually, I'm glad I missed those particular weeks) and being able to chat to Anna and my family. Anna and I had spoken every night since we met, and I always looked forward to hearing her voice. And I tell my parents everything about my life, so it seemed impossible to believe I wouldn't be able to talk to them again until I'd either crashed out of the game or I'd got to the final. And even if I got to the final, I could still be calling with bad news.

I was allowed to reveal to the people closest to me that I was on the show (everyone else thought I was going on an Army operation), and when I told my dad, he said that I technically had a 1-in-22 chance of winning the £120k, which would be great odds at the horse racing, but was still no guarantee of anything. All it took was one person to dislike me and encourage others to gang up on me, and I'd be gone. Mum and Anna said they thought I was going to be sent back straight away, because (as I mentioned in the introduction), I'm a terrible liar and have the worst poker face in the world. But they both know me far too well to be taken in by a fib, whereas these people I was going to meet in Scotland didn't know me at all. I was determined to make sure that remained the case. I really wanted to win the game, and I had a plan to help me do just that.

As the train sped on, I remembered something I'd been told in the Army: if you can't be good, be careful. I'd held onto that ever since, and I knew it was going to be useful here. In fact, in that moment, it seemed that everything I'd ever learnt—in my childhood, through my family, in church, in school, in the Army, and even at my lowest moment, lying on that bed in hospital—had been preparing me for this moment. It felt like destiny.

Maybe it wasn't nerves that were making me shake. Maybe it was excitement.

The first person I met was Paul. It was the following day, and all the contestants had boarded a train together, so we could have some initial conversations. Paul was sitting opposite me, and I noticed he was dressed in the same kind of clothing. We looked at each other and sort of smiled. My first impression of him as a person, though, wasn't great. I didn't hate him, but I thought he was way too cocky and sure of himself. Obviously, now I'm aware of his game plan, I realise he wasn't particularly smug at all. Paul went into *The Traitors* determined to have fun, and the most fun he thought he could have was by playing the villain. I saw the evil side of him (game recognises game), but I had to admit that he carried it off very well, chatting to and being charming to everyone. I didn't trust him, and believed I'd definitely have to find a way to get rid of him, but I did think 'this guy is a vibe' and I knew straight away that if there was anyone I wanted to be a Traitor with, it would be Paul.

Then Tracey, who I came to call my second mum, sat down with us. Paul was asking loads of questions, and I was trying to answer, but I just couldn't get over where I was. The train was proper posh, with tea and booths and everything, and we were going through the most beautiful Scottish countryside. Some of the contestants were absorbed in trying to suss everyone out, looking around, checking for dodgy behaviour, asking really invasive questions, which was silly because we didn't even have our roles yet. They'd probably watched season 1 too many times, taken too many notes and thought way too hard about things, and that was never going to help. My game plan was just to go in there, roll with the punches and control what I could. Worrying about anything else seemed silly, as the whole thing would probably be chaos anyway. The best I could do was keep my head down and make sure people trusted me.

The only problem would be being a Faithful, because you have so little control; you can wake up one morning and just be told that you're dead. But as I had no idea what was going to happen in the game or what role the show was going to give me, I did what I could in that moment and just let go.

Looking out the window, I felt like Harry Potter, hopefully about to make some mischief.

Arriving at our destination was the most surreal thing ever. You're standing outside a huge medieval castle, there's a *Traitors* flag flying from a flagpole, there are bloody peacocks walking around and, strangest of all, the weather was amazing (it stayed that way for almost the entire four weeks we were in Scotland). When we were all lined up outside the castle entrance, things began to feel a lot more serious. It's hard to say why exactly, but when Claudia Winkleman walked out, I thought she was one of the most powerful women I'd ever seen. She has this amazing aura about her. And obviously the best dress sense in the Scottish Highlands. I'd spent years watching *Strictly* with my mum and dad, and now here was Claudia herself, talking to us and telling us about the game. As our first challenge, she asked us all to get in a line in order of how likely we thought we were to win or lose. Straight away, I slotted into the middle. I knew there weren't many people around my age playing, and my plan was to be young, dumb and sort of gullible. Being on either end of the line wasn't going to do me any favours in that. I was confused by the people who put themselves on as the most or least likely: either you look like you think too much of yourself or too little, and in neither case are people likely to respect you.

Then we all went inside and I got to work . . . The moment I met someone, I began to create an imaginary pinboard with their name and how I might get rid of them if necessary, for example, this guy's all 'Team, Team, Team'; he's trying too hard; this woman's too quiet; she's trying to fly under the radar, and so on. I don't think I switched off for the whole four weeks. I knew if I lost concentration, I'd make a mistake, and my Army training taught me to always be ready. It gave me a good grounding for what was about to come.

Diane was the first person I wanted to have on my side. She's fiercely intelligent and knows how to handle herself, and I wanted to make sure I wasn't ever up against her, because I felt she could go after me. In fact, before our first round table, she looked me straight in the eye and asked who I thought the Traitors were.

When we all sat down at the table for the first time, I had Diane on one side and Zack on the other. We put on our blindfolds so Claudia could touch the Traitors on the shoulder and let them know they'd been chosen. Cheeky as I am, I tried to sneak a peek, but it was impossible—all I could go on was the sound of Claudia's footsteps as she walked round and round, her boots knocking slowly on the floor. It was honestly the most tense thing, and Zack began to breathe really heavily. My heart was beating fast too, and in that moment, I almost didn't want to be a Traitor. I wasn't sure I could stand the pressure of feeling like this every single night! But the second I felt Claudia's hand squeeze my shoulder, my nerves disappeared. I was going to get to play my game and have some fun, and it was the best feeling ever.

After a long, long time in the dark, Claudia told us to take our blindfolds off. The light was almost blinding, and at that moment, I felt that if anyone spoke to me, I would crack. I didn't feel comfortable at all. Normally, I'm really good at compartmentalising (as I've explained), and I'd been planning to act like a Faithful until I put my Traitor's cloak on. But it was only a minute since I'd discovered my plan was actually working out, and I wasn't quite ready mentally . . . Then bang! What's the first thing that happens? Diane turns to me and asks me if I'm all right, thinking the heavy breathing was mine. She then asks what's changed and whether I'm a Traitor. I managed to shake that off, saying that nothing's changed and that it was Zack who was breathing heavily. I'm not sure she's convinced, and I keep catching her looking over, trying to work me out.

That was when I knew I had to take Diane down. I just had to find the right moment.

Getting through the next few hours without saying something stupid was nerve-wracking, but somehow I managed it. Then, when the sky was pitch black, I walked out into the misty courtyard and saw Claudia illuminated by firelight, holding my Traitor's cloak. I remember saying something about how I was going to win this game, and she laughed as I walked into the turret and said, 'Happy Murdering'. And she was right; it was going to be happy.

The second I put my cloak on and obscured my face with the hood, I felt a sense of power. My naughty side was coming out, and I was excited to get going, but it felt as if I'd spent ages alone in the turret when I finally heard the sound of the door opening. Looking down, I saw two large feet enter and stride across the floor. I guessed they must belong to Miles or Paul, as they were the biggest guys around, and I really hoped they were Paul's. I thought that would be the coolest thing ever. The second we took our hoods off, we burst out laughing and knew this was going to be so much fun. Then there was another knock and more delicate footsteps tapped across the metal floor . . . they were soon revealed to belong to Ash.

I began to size up my fellow Traitors. In every group, there's a hierarchy, and naturally, there was one in the turret. My feeling was that Ash was going to get herself caught in this game. Her plan seemed to be to move around the castle and make friends with everyone, but that made it look as if she was doing too much. Sonja got suspicious, and at the first breakfast, asked Ash point-blank if she was a Traitor, which Ash denied, though not convincingly. From that moment on, Paul and I knew we needed to watch her. Though our aim was for the three of us to get to the end of the game together, we were aware that at some point we might need a scapegoat . . . and there was no harm at all in having one in the turret.

As for Paul, I was happy to let him think he was at the top of the hierarchy. Maybe believing he was the evil mastermind pulling the strings would make him feel comfortable enough to (inadvertently) shoot himself in the foot.

Those first few days were amazing. We got Aubrey and Kyra out without anyone blinking, and we managed to banish Sonja, which was great, as she seemed quite a formidable player. Brian, well . . . Brian kind of banished himself. Never seen an innocent man act so guilty.

Even better was that we recruited Miles. Miles was really influential in the group—he was a laugh and a great person, but we knew he also had a cheeky, mischievous side to him, which meant we could probably persuade him to be naughty. At the same time, we had something on him. Miles didn't get involved in challenges, which made him look as if he had no need for the protection of a shield, and he never spoke out strongly against anyone at the round tables, seeming to prefer to sit back and stay out of the hunt for Traitors. We knew that, if we needed to, we could accuse him of being comfortable watching other people go at each other, and it was unlikely he'd be able to argue or fight back well.

We also recruited Miles because, though it's great to keep reducing the numbers of Faithfuls, it's handy to have someone you can push things onto, and I think Paul and I both felt there was a chance we might need another Traitor fairly soon. Heads were turning towards Ash, and after a few accusations over a few days, some people were gunning for her. She wasn't doing a good enough job of convincing the group, and Paul and I knew there was no space for weakness in the team. On the fourth night, when Claudia asked everyone to write their nomination for banishment, Paul looked over at me. We knew what had to be done, and though it was tough turning on Ash, that's the game. No one wants to be seen to be defending a Traitor.

Despite us both writing down her name, Ash survived the vote that night, which made for the most awkward turret meeting ever. There was silence for a very long time, broken only by Paul doing his evil laugh in an effort to relieve the tension. What do you say to someone who just doesn't see things as you do? We felt we'd played as we needed to win; she regarded what we'd done as a betrayal, and that was why she was so shocked. In the turret, we had all promised our loyalty to one another, to being Traitors together and to carrying each other to the final.

But one of the biggest mistakes you can make in *The Traitors* is to take it too seriously. That night, Ash finally realised it was a game we were playing, and that we weren't going to pander to her feelings when there was £120k at stake. Paul and I were out for ourselves.

It's tricky: you have to not trust anyone, but at the same time, if you don't trust some people, that's going to get you too. For now, and while we had a weaker player in the turret, Paul and I trusted each other. But when Ash realised that Paul and I weren't going to save her, she knew she had to do something big herself to get back.

That's when Claudia told us about the dungeon.

For anyone who doesn't remember, dungeon week was when the Traitors had to pick four players to go down to the dungeon for the day while everyone else did a challenge. These four 'Condemned' players would be the only ones who could be murdered by the Traitors, barring one, who the remaining group could vote to save from this fate. Ash wanted to put herself in the dungeon to try and clear her name, which made sense, as on paper, it made her look marginally less guilty. At the same time, all it took was for someone to float the idea that there was a Traitor in the dungeon, and before long, everyone might be looking at the Condemned players as potential Traitors.

As I was pretty sure this would happen, I felt going down there would be to draw attention to yourself unnecessarily. And in this sense, Paul played things badly by joining Ash. We knew that the most popular player would get out of the dungeon and, as a popular guy, Paul was ready to assume that that would be him. I'm not sure if he thought he was cleverer than other people and better at pulling the strings; probably, he just felt that going down to the dungeon offered the most fun, because if he survived this, he'd be even more of the evil genius he was playing. He'd picked that character part for himself, and he loved it.

I thought his move was the stupidest thing ever, but it was his idea. To be honest, I always felt Paul would stitch himself up.

All I had to do was keep my mouth shut and watch it happen.

When Andrew was picked to be saved from murder by the group, both Paul and Ash were in trouble. As Claudia pointed out on the show, if Meg had been banished that night, then the only two people who could be murdered by the Traitors were Paul and Ash, and when they both came down to breakfast the next morning, their Traitor status would have been obvious.

At the round table, when the spotlight came onto Paul and he broke down, saying the whole process was taking it out of him, I knew his distress was coming from something real. We'd talked a lot about how much we missed our loved ones. Being in the Army, I'd gotten used to being apart from the people I care about, but Paul had spent every day for the last 13 years with Kate, his amazing wife, and now they had a baby boy, Charlie, who was just a few months old. Being away from them both had taken something out of him and, even though his emotional outburst helpfully deflected attention (and I do think Paul's a great actor), I knew he was speaking the truth too. Either way, it worked.

Ash was not so lucky. The whispers of a Traitor being in the dungeon became shouts, and when it came to the vote, Paul and I weren't the only ones who put her name on our slates.

With Ash's banishment, the group got their first Traitor, and so did we. Ash was gone and couldn't come back at us. We'd kept the numbers in the turret up, and we'd killed off a lot of people. And no one suspected me.

Not even Paul.

12

THE TRAITORS: PART II

EVEN WHEN I WATCHED the show back later, I thought Paul was great. He had all the right answers under fire; he managed what people in the group thought of him really well, and everyone just seemed to love him. Based on what I witnessed in the turret, I knew he could be an evil mastermind, but none of the Faithfuls ever saw that: to them, he was just a soft, nice, unassuming guy. That was a little bit of a challenge for me. You see, you have to choose your moment very carefully if you want to take down one of the popular guys, because you're going against public opinion. And at that stage, no one really suspected Paul. No one except Jaz.

After Ash was banished, the Traitors had a great run. First, we murdered Meg, then Jonny was banished, then we got Tracey (sorry Tracey!), and then Anthony was voted out by the team. Two days of pure Traitors mayhem and, for me, two days closer to the final.

Then, one evening, Jaz pulled me aside and told me secretively about his suspicions over Paul. I could see he wasn't too sure if this was a smart move, and of course, I passed the message on to Paul. Neither of us was really worried, though, because we didn't see Jaz as a threat.

In any social group, sub-groups tend to develop, and that's what happened on *The Traitors*. As I've already suggested, when you can trust no one, you move closer to the people you feel you can trust a little more—they might be around your age, or have similar ideas about things as you.

In our year, there were three major groups: the 'Elder Group', which was Aubrey, Diane, Tracey and Sonja; the 'London Gang', which was Jasmine, Ross, Zack and Mollie; and the 'Removal Men', which was Paul, Anthony, Andrew and me. (I think Anthony once called us that because we did so much of the heavy lifting in the challenges, and the name stuck.)

There were pros and cons to being part of a group. If you were a member, you knew that when it got to a round table, the others in your group would trust your response was genuine (or at least give you the benefit of the doubt) when the accusations started flying around. Also, at times when you really had no clue what was going on, those connections could feel invaluable. But then, as we'll see with the London Gang, if trust among group members was broken, the whole thing could collapse.

It's a tricky balance to strike, but if you want to win, you have to be your own person while at the same time relying on and believing in others.

In the show when it came out, Jaz was made out to look like the ultimate detective, but my view of him was completely different. Jaz never joined a group or made friends or got close to people because, as he admits, he didn't trust anyone. I think this was his big mistake.

You see, when it came to saying at the round table that you suspected a person, you had to show you had some reason to do so—some knowledge or evidence to back yourself up, because random accusations never landed. I always say that 25% of *The Traitors* is thinking about who could be a Traitor; 25% is presenting a reasonably convincing argument; 25% is persuading people of your view, and the final 25% is bringing enough of the group round so you can actually get rid of that person. I worked this out early on, and when I went for someone, I really tried to give the full 100%

Jaz could have been the best detective ever if he'd followed a similar strategy, but he could never convince people, particularly as he acted more like a Traitor than the Traitors themselves. As he didn't trust anyone, he'd go against the group in missions, and because he only followed his own gut, he would ignore mounting evidence and just go for the person he suspected, which would largely mean he voted for someone random without anyone else knowing why. So, while Jaz may have had some good ideas, he was never able to win over the group.

Looking back, the Traitors had control of that season all the way through. If someone went, it was because of us, and this meant a Traitor could only be taken down by one of their own.

Hard as it is to admit, I think Anthony (my fellow Removal Man) and Jonny were affected by similar issues to those affecting Jaz. Anthony didn't do enough to convince people he wasn't a Traitor, and Jonny simply didn't have enough people on his side. I couldn't argue to keep him in, because I saw the writing was on the wall. And so, I was part of the group that got Jonny out.

His banishment was definitely one of the most difficult to cope with because Jonny was basically my hero. We were both Army guys, and this gave us a shared view of the world and an instant connection. Straight away, when we met, we spoke about the military and told each other our stories and about where we'd been. He seemed like a brother to me, and speaking to him was probably the closest to home I felt during those four weeks away. But while we were really similar, he'd served in a way I don't feel I ever did, and I was in total admiration of him for that. He was a veteran who had been deployed to Afghanistan and genuinely fought for our country. He had lost a leg in the course of his service over there.

We had a great connection and really bonded, but at the same time, he was such a smart guy that I saw him as a danger to me. Fortunately, everyone had decided—with no solid reason—that he needed to go, and it would have looked way more suspicious for me if I hadn't jumped on that bandwagon. But voting Jonny out took its toll. I had to walk off afterwards because I had a lot going on in my head . . . I do remember telling myself that I couldn't dwell on what had happened; that I just had to get up and keep going as the Army had taught me. I'm sure Jonny would have understood.

After Anthony's banishment, there was a lot of anger and frustration in the group. I can't imagine how confusing it must be to be sure in yourself that someone is a Traitor and then for that person to turn around and tell you they're a Faithful. Everyone must have felt so bad, and I think the guilt of depriving someone innocent of the chance to win £120,000 was also playing on people's minds. Each contestant on *The Traitors* has an amazing personal story to tell and a good reason for wanting to win the money, so if you kill or banish them, you know you're stopping them from carrying out whatever great plans they had.

In the midst of this chaos, I was actually growing in confidence. More and more people were beginning to trust me; I had better connections with people in the group (especially, at this point, Zack, Mollie and Ross), and one of my biggest threats, Jonny, was now gone.

Maybe because we were doing so well, the show threw us a curveball. Rather than murdering someone from a distance from the turret, we had to give our chosen victim a poisoned chalice to drink from, in front of everyone. Paul, Miles and I needed to quickly concoct a plan, and we met outside by the fire pit. I'm not going to lie; we were all panicking a little bit. We'd never had to do this to someone in real life, and the fear of being caught was obviously playing on us. But I saw—and took—the opportunity to push for Diane . . . There was a chance she still had my number, and so she needed to go. Paul and Miles went along with the plan. But though I manipulated things so we'd choose the right victim, there was no way I was going to be seen anywhere near the scene of the crime. I volunteered quickly to be the person to find the chalice, before handing it over to one of the others to do the deed. For some reason, Miles said he'd give the chalice to Diane. I'm not sure if he knew it at the time, but that was a terrible move. I set myself up well there. Paul was equally happy to be largely uninvolved.

Not very many things disconcert you as a Traitor, and I had no idea that one of the most shocking moments of the show was about to play out . . . Miles had managed to give

Diane the chalice the evening before, and the next morning, the three of us got up and went to breakfast. We were sitting around that amazing table, eating, and drinking our coffees, the sun streaming in through the windows (again, crazy weather for Scotland), quietly congratulating ourselves on how well things had gone.

And at that moment, Diane walks in.

I couldn't believe it.

I played it pretty cool, I think (you never know with my poker face), but when I looked at Miles and Paul, I could tell they were thinking the same thing . . . Did we do it wrong? How else could we have applied the poison? What on earth is going on?

Then, Claudia appears and explains that someone's been poisoned and they will be dead by the end of the day (which was a big relief for me). And the second Claudia leaves the room, Paul starts planning to topple Miles . . .

Diane's funeral was amazing. It was one of the most haunting, weirdest days ever. And apart from the fact that my allergy to horses meant I could barely speak without sneezing, I was actually loving it. Because the group was panicking and liable to start throwing wild accusations, Paul and I felt we had to raise people's suspicions about Miles. Paul had already planted some seeds that morning, saying Miles had given Diane a drink, and I was happy to water those seeds. If someone has got heat on them and you feel they might be discovered, you don't want it to seem as if you're trying to protect them. So, Paul and I decided to look like we were hunting for a Traitor—and this felt like the perfect moment to get rid of one.

After the funeral, which was really tense and emotionally draining for many of the contestants (including, apparently, Ross), people were out for blood. And Paul supplied it. He really went for Miles and even tried to convince everyone that Diane had told him that if she was murdered, Miles would be the one responsible. It was risky, as Paul's argument was thin and he was relying on words no one could prove, given that Diane was dead. Eventually, though, Paul swayed the group, and when Miles revealed he was a Traitor, we all cheered. But Paul had stuck his neck out. Like before, he had assumed the group would instantly back him and they hadn't, so in the long battle between them, Miles had got some good shots in, holes had been picked in Paul's argument, and I'd even had the chance to lean over to Zack and ask him if he thought this looked like two Traitors going at each other.

Miles went, Paul celebrated, and I learned a valuable lesson. If you're going to put someone in the ground, do it quickly.

Nowadays, people ask me how I could so easily betray people on the show. I think they assume that I must be some kind of psycho, and as I've mentioned, I do have what I call my 'Jekyll and Hyde switch', where I can go from acting in one way to acting in another way entirely. Sometimes, when I was playing Monopoly with my family, I'd be the Banker. In that role, I felt I could stick my hand in the till every so often and get a quick £500. But the second I stopped being the Banker, I'd just be the Old Shoe again, trying to build my empire, so it didn't really feel as if I was doing anything wrong. It made sense to me to put these different roles in two different places in my head.

In the turret, I loved being a Traitor, but the second I took my cloak off, I'd tell myself I was a Faithful. Ultimately, acting in a certain way is half the game; the other half is getting people to believe in you.

As I was one of the youngest contestants, I knew the others were likely to assume I hadn't achieved very much, and I was happy to appear as immature—the fun, bubbly class clown who people wouldn't take too seriously. Also, as I tend not to think before I speak—which I put down to my dyslexia and the fact that my brain is wired differently—I sometimes come out with the most random stuff, and this does, admittedly, make me seem a little stupid.

In fact (as you know), I have a huge amount of life experience from the Army and leaving home at sixteen. And, while I'm not great with general knowledge and may not seem book-smart, when it comes to high-pressure environments, I thrive.

I never minded playing dumb, because I wanted people to underestimate me (and Paul, amongst others, was doing just that). I genuinely think it's the most dangerous thing you can do, so I try never to do it myself, but in this case, Paul misjudging me fitted perfectly with my game plan. As I know, I'm clever in lots of ways, and playing a role doesn't change my view of myself. With Andrew, it was a different story.

Andrew is the nicest guy ever and a real friendly giant. He was into rugby before he suffered a car crash, which left him unable to play the game ever again. He admitted to us all that there was a period of his life when, because of the injuries he suffered, he felt unsure of himself and just had no confidence. Now, though, he's pushed through and wears his scars like a warrior. He even helps others with their own mental health struggles, and I admire him so much for all of that.

Naturally, because he was so honest about everything and because he's a great team player (probably from rugby), for a while, Andrew was one of the most popular people in the group. On the first day, he made a lovely speech about the pleasure it was to be here with us all, and how he was looking forward to getting to know everyone. Initially, at least, that put him in quite a position of power.

On my pinboard, though, I had a note that Andrew was, if anything, too much of a team player. Everything was about the team. He would raise his glass and make a toast to celebrate the day, even after we'd voted out a Faithful. I knew I could easily make it look as if he was trying too hard, almost overcompensating for something, and I wasn't the only person who began noticing this. After Miles got banished, Andrew had some heat on him, so I knew who I wanted to join us in the turret.

However, although Paul and I both felt that Andrew would be a good recruit, there was a problem: being recruited wasn't such a good thing for Andrew. He realised that he'd been brought in as a scapegoat and his behaviour changed instantly, both in the turret and within the group. Day by day, he got more and more annoyed and frustrated with everything. In his heart, he was a team player who wanted to help everyone, so being a Traitor went completely against how he felt he should act. Essentially, it went against his morals. And because he couldn't approach being a Traitor as, in effect, playing a role, he did the worst thing you can possibly do when you become a Traitor, which is to tell yourself you need to act like a Traitor.

But the best Traitors are the ones who act like Faithfuls.

Paul seemed really happy with how Andrew was acting, probably because he thought it took the heat off him. But I was still hearing Paul's name around a lot. I would mention to him that this or that person seemed to find what he did suspicious, but he never seemed to take these comments on board and mostly just laughed.

On the day Paul decided to put himself in the dungeon, I was asking around to see who people thought we should aim for at the round table, when someone mentioned that Paul had been planting some seeds about me. I didn't think he was actively going for me right then and there, but I could tell he was laying the groundwork, and I knew I needed to shut things down as soon as possible.

Paul and I were really close and had so much fun together, first, because we saw the game the same way; and second, because we shared a secret and spent literally hours in the turret with each other, plotting and planning. All the contestants from season 2 have a WhatsApp group, and it was fun to be a part of that when the show was aired, but Paul's the one I made a real, lasting connection with. I'd have loved to go all the way to the final with him. But if he was going to start coming for me, then I would have to fight back. And as close as we were, this was just another day in the office. I started preparing my argument for that night.

There was so much evidence stacking up against Paul that my speaking against him wouldn't come as a shock to the group. All I needed was someone to challenge him, but this was not for the faint-hearted, because Paul was really good at responding and always seemed to have the perfect answer to anything. He could even make you doubt yourself and wonder whether you were right for asking in the first place.

As we sat down, I felt quite calm. I knew I had to give Paul the full 100% but to do so in a way that wouldn't look as if I was making too much of a direct attack, I'd have to wait for someone to bring up his name. That happened fairly quickly, and I immediately took my opportunity. A confused look went over Paul's face as I began with 'This sets me up perfectly . . .' I knew if I let him respond before I said my piece, he might have me, so I just threw everything at him in one go. I talked about how he didn't let people have a chance to think or even breathe when he was being accused and how that seemed like a massive overcompensation; I mentioned how he only appeared to stick his neck out when people ended up being Traitors which was suspicious in itself; I explained how I thought he messed up in the dungeon (using my insider knowledge to colour the details); and I ended by going at him for bringing up names and sowing seeds about other players, some of whom, I knew, weren't going to be happy even to be mentioned and weren't going to take that well at all. I could see he was quite shocked, and I think he was imagining how he could quickly respond persuasively to all my accusations, if he wanted to claw things back at all.

But the fight seemed to go out of him. I was aware he missed his family massively, and even now, when we speak, he says he'd already had enough and was excited to go back and see his baby boy. He knew his game had come to an end, but he wasn't bitter about it, and that's why we're still friends.

Another year, I genuinely think Paul could have won. He was such a good player, and there was a reason he lasted so long. He gave people proper belly laughs all the time, and he told, and still tells, the best stories ever. He made some tactical errors along the way, but he says he has no regrets about how he played, that he enjoyed the game so much and wouldn't do anything differently. And, as Grandad Dave used to say when we were boxing, I think that's all that matters.

Paul also tells me that before he left, he saw Claudia one last time. And he said to her, 'Harry needs to go on and win the show.'

Now I just had to make that happen.

13

THE TRAITORS: PART III

LIFE IN THE TURRET was weird without Paul. I know it's ironic to say this, but out of everyone, I trusted Paul the most, and I only realised that after he was gone. Andrew definitely didn't seem to be enjoying Traitor life as much, and besides, he'd just watched me betray Paul, so I'm not sure he really trusted me either. The smart thing for him to do would have been to target me, but he knew I played the game well, so he seemed content for me to carry on with the planning.

Of course, you could never be sure where an accusation was going to come from, and with fewer people now taking part (though still a good many between me and the final), there was more chance I would fall under the spotlight.

I had to think of something big.

After we got rid of Paul, everyone went to the bar to celebrate. They were all thrilled with me, calling me 'The Traitor Hunter' and telling me that I was on the Faithful throne. You'd think I'd love it, everyone basically chanting my name, but I was wary of the attention and worried it was putting me too much at the forefront of people's minds. It totally went against my plan to fly under the radar. Also, the way I saw it—and the way I was worried other people would see it—was if I was The Traitor Hunter and I was a Faithful, the smart thing for the Traitors to do would be to murder me that night.

But I'd always had a plan for that situation. The reason I worked so hard in the challenges was so that if anyone turned round and asked why I was still here, I could just say because I gave my all in every mission. If you were a Traitor, you'd be silly to get rid of me, as I was winning you money (at the end of the day, everyone—Faithful or Traitor—wanted to build up that pot.) I had a whole speech prepared and did have to use bits of it once or twice. Ultimately, though, at this stage, no one knew why they were still there. So many theories and plans and ideas were being thrown around every day, it was impossible to keep track of everything. And if you were a Faithful, trying to work out what the Traitors were doing was just guesswork anyway.

Paul was the only person anyone had any real evidence for, and once he was gone, the euphoria dissipated, and we were back to chaos. But Traitors thrive in chaos. Andrew and I chose to murder Charlie because no one had any issues with her and would find her demise unsettlingly random. The group was basically back to going off gut feeling. But that tended to result in random votes, which could be dangerous. The way I saw it, as a Traitor, it was my job to provide them with evidence. It was time for a recruitment.

One of the ways in which the Traitors definitely have an advantage in the game is that they know how many Traitors there are, whereas not knowing makes being a Faithful really hard. I wanted to take advantage of that. The group had managed to oust Miles and Paul in quick succession, and while there was a chance people thought there might be two more Traitors lurking around, I was pretty sure that no one would suspect there were three. However, in order to recruit someone to join Andrew and me, I needed somehow to mask the lack of a murder.

I could pretend that winning *The Traitors* was entirely down to skill, but the truth is I had a whole lot of luck along the way. I got lucky that Ash never tried to throw any of us under the bus (which she could easily have done); I got lucky that Miles and Andrew both agreed to join us as Traitors; I got lucky that no one ever really had a strong enough feeling it was me (which could have happened at any moment); and my next stroke of luck was Ross's recruitment (of which more soon . . .)

The day Charlie failed to come down for breakfast, we were given our next challenge. We had to go to Claudia's cabin in the woods, which turned out to involve clambering through loads of disgusting tunnels underneath the floor. Even though I like being clean, the Army taught me not to mind getting dirty, so I got stuck in. But I wasn't really focused on the dirt. I was looking around for one thing in particular. Suddenly, in the dark, I saw it glinting . . .

I knew if I got the shield and managed to keep that a secret, I could pretend the Traitors had tried to murder me in the night but failed, which was the perfect cover for a recruitment. So, I quickly reached my hand in, dislodged the shield and put it straight in my pocket. The only person who saw what I'd done was Mollie, which was another bit of luck, as she trusted me completely. I put my finger to my lips to ask her to keep quiet, and I knew she would.

That was just the first part of the plan, though. I realised that if I only told a select number of people I had the shield, then I could accuse those who didn't know of trying to murder me. Before our round table that night, I confided in Jaz and Zack. Those two were going to help me frame some innocent Faithfuls.

As I've said, no one really trusted Jaz, so framing him was pointless. He just happened to be in the room when I was revealing my find, and I didn't mind him knowing, but my real target for that piece of information was Zack.

Zack was my secret weapon in the game. At the first round table, I'd voted for him, partly to convince Diane that it was Zack and not me who had been breathing heavily. I don't think anyone blamed me for voting for Zack, as he was a hard guy to figure out. After that, I didn't ever vote for him again, and we became quite close. Having Zack on my side ended up being like a superpower for me. He had done really well at working out the game, and now he would come to me with his thoughts and clues. We became a little team.

Some people never got on board with Zack, and most of the group, at some point, were suspicious of him, but actually, he was the first to tell me about Paul, and he said he thought Andrew was dodgy almost straight after we recruited him. He was rarely wrong and almost a perfect Faithful, except that when he had a gut feeling and thought he'd worked something out, he didn't care what anyone else thought.

Zack was great for me because I could feed him the information I wanted him to have and then watch him run with it without getting involved. So, after imparting the clues he would need about the shield and my 'attempted murder', I left him to put the puzzle together himself. It wasn't his fault that it was missing one key piece.

That evening, the confusion in the group caused another wrong banishment, and I was free to recruit.

Ross already had some heat on him, and that was helpful for me, but so too was the fact that the London Gang were beginning to fight. They had quickly become a group in the first week and, as much as you could be, were friends who trusted one another. This had helped them get to these later stages. However, when you're part of a group and someone from that group throws an accusation at you, you take it way more personally. Over the last couple of days, Zack had fired shots at Jasmine, which she really didn't appreciate, so she was firing pretty hard back.

While this was happening, Ross wasn't sure who to believe and kept bouncing between Zack and Jasmine, and the fact that he was failing to show any allegiance meant no one was on his side.

Also, he hadn't done very well at hunting Traitors. He believed in Paul until the end and stuck his neck out to lynch lots of people, including Jonny, who turned out to be a Faithful. So, that night, as I always did, I recruited someone I knew I could get rid of if need be . . .

When Ross entered the turret, I could tell he was coming quite reluctantly. After all, because of us, he'd had to put a rose in his own mum's coffin. Then, hilariously, I made a fairly harsh comment about Diane, and when I watched the show later on, I discovered that Ross said to camera at this point that he was going to take any chance he could to get us back. He was right not to trust us, but I think the reason he wanted to go after us was more emotional than tactical.

At that point, of course, I had no idea that Diane was his mum, but after the confusion about her possibly being

Paul's, some of us were on the lookout for relationships between others in the group. I do think Ross and Diane made the game harder for themselves by going in as mother and son. I don't know how they did it, or why they did it. Straight away, they couldn't truly be themselves. And getting angry (as Ross did) because someone had said something derogatory about another player in the game (Diane), just made the whole thing way more complicated.

Still, they did come in together. I murdered Diane, I made Ross go to his own mum's funeral, and now Ross had a plan to get me. Which was fine, because I had a plan to get him.

The next day, when we all walked into the breakfast room, you could see people were struggling to work out what was going on. That's when I made my big reveal. I told everyone I had the shield and that the Traitors must have tried to murder me. Straight away, Zack began his campaign, and this served to distract those who hadn't known I had the shield from considering whether I might be lying and if there had actually been a recruitment. People trusted me as a Faithful, which meant that Ross, Jasmine and Evie were now in the firing line . . . with Zack after them.

For our challenge that day, we had to split off into teams and answer puzzles, and as I'm just not good with words, I immediately got caught out. I ran over to the scroll, as instructed, thinking the worst thing that could happen was that I'd get pulled up into the sky by a massive net, but instead I plunged into a horrible, black puddle covered with leaves. It was so well camouflaged, it basically looked like the ground, and I went head first. It was freezing cold in there, and the mud got in my hair, which was gross. I was not happy. And then I had to wait around in my wet, dirty clothes for everyone to finish the challenge.

What made the whole day better, though, was that no one got the shield. You can see on the show that I had a cheeky smile on my face when Claudia told us that. Now, everyone was fair game.

The shield was really useful, but it overcomplicated things for everyone. It protects you, so getting it once or twice is fine and makes it seem as if you're just happy to survive. However, if you get it too many times, it looks as if you're actually a Traitor and double-bluffing, or trying to get the shield so no one else can. Zack would always see the other side of the coin (well, apart from my trick) and would be the first to say someone's trying too hard for the shield and call them out on it.

You also had to bear in mind that being a team player and working with everyone to get money for the pot was a much better look than obsessing over getting the shield. In the first ever challenge, Kyra went straight for the shield, and no one appreciated that. The Traitors could have left the group to pull her apart, but she took control of things a little too much, and we could see she might be a threat, so we murdered her ourselves.

And now, weeks later, we were coming up to the final. I was delighted that no one had the shield and could feel myself within touching distance of the end. All I needed to do was to survive tonight, murder someone before tomorrow, get through the last round table, and I'd be there . . . possibly even with a group of people I knew I could beat.

The perfect scenario for any Traitor is to have two people going at each other at the round table. Then the vote tends to be between those two, as they've been pulling the other's game apart in front of the group, and once one of them is revealed to be a Faithful, everyone turns on the other. All you have to do when this is happening is to sit back, not get involved, and cast your vote based on what everyone else on the table is saying. Then you'll survive another day, or even two, if the accuser quickly goes as well.

I knew that with a few carefully sown seeds, I could guide the next couple of banishments. Jasmine and Zack were already fighting, and after my reveal about the shield and Zack's deduction that the Traitor must be either Jasmine or Evie, they were starting to point fingers at each other, too. They both knew that they were innocent, so they assumed the other one must be guilty. And Zack was suspicious of Ross, whether because of Ross's voting record or because he never backed Zack against Jasmine. The only people who weren't in some kind of battle were me, Jaz and Mollie, and I wanted to keep it that way.

Ross's big mistake was to give me a seed to sow between him and Andrew. In the run-up to his first round table as a Traitor that night, Ross told me Andrew had said to him that I was being elusive. There was a chance Ross was lying, and I knew the easiest way to find out was to air things in public. The best thing possible happened. It turned out that Andrew *had* said what Ross claimed, but when I mentioned this at the round table, Andrew flagrantly denied this, making it look as if Ross was doing his own seed-sowing. Ross's reaction to Andrew's denial was so strong that the group started to believe Andrew might actually be lying. When you can't trust anyone, not being sure whether someone is telling the truth or not makes that person seem very suspicious—and

Ross and Andrew were each making the other appear that way. Meanwhile, Jasmine and Evie were going at each other, and Zack was stoking the fire.

That night, Ross was banished, making me look better for catching him out. People had begun to suspect Andrew, because of Ross's reaction. Evie and Jasmine were still in the frame for apparently trying to murder me, and I knew that my next move would make them look even more guilty. I had to murder Zack.

The Traitors took place over four weeks, but it felt like six months. There was so much happening. You'd be talking to everyone in the group, all day, every day, about everything in your life, as well as doing extreme things, quite outside most people's experience. It did mean you got close to your fellow contestants and, as I've mentioned, one of those I was closest to was Zack.

He was honestly invaluable to my game. Paul helped out a lot, too—his game was like a stepping stone that took me across the river. Similarly, Jonny didn't rat me out straight away or point a finger when he could have, and his banishment gave me a chance to spread my wings.

But right from the beginning, I knew that no matter how close I got to people, if I didn't make the necessary moves at the right time, I would never win. So even though I didn't really want to, I knew I had to murder Zack. He was great, but he was also a threat; the only double-bluff he hadn't considered in the whole game was that I was lying about the shield, and that was because he trusted me so much. However, if the second Jasmine and Evie turned out not to be Traitors, things would fall apart, so I needed to get rid of him before they went. And they would go if Zack went, as he had been the one accusing them both.

As I'd planned, at our round table that day, the group voted off Jasmine. This must have been painful for Evie, because even though she was now in the final, she had pointed the finger strongly at Faithful Jasmine, and everyone was going to believe now that Evie herself was the Traitor.

So, there was a deflated kind of feeling in the room after Jasmine's banishment. Then, Claudia revealed she'd set up a meal for us five finalists to enjoy together. As we walked out, no one seemed to think getting dressed up and sitting down with people you felt so uncomfortable around was going to be anything but weird. Ross had been caught the previous evening, but the Faithfuls knew there was at least one more Traitor in the game, and no one trusted anyone. As Evie said in her interview, who wants to have dinner with a bunch of people you think might be out to get you? And even though I was excited about how everything had come together, this meal felt like a trap because another evening was another chance to get caught. I was ready for this whole process to be over.

In the end, though, the meal turned out to be fun. The room was huge and posh and lit by loads of candles. I think we all felt tense when we walked in, but after we'd sat down and had a glass of wine, we began sharing stories. In spite of the fact that tomorrow only one group (or even one person) could walk away with the money, we were soon laughing and chatting away about everything we'd been through—and we had, after all, been through a lot. The challenges, the round tables, the banishments, the breakfasts, the chats, the whispers and the games. Andrew made one of his toasts, and, as on the first day, it actually felt as if it brought us all closer together.

The others left one by one, and I ended up in the dimly lit room by myself. In the silence, I thought about how, if I wanted to get the money, these would be the people I'd have to win it off. But that had been the case throughout the competition, and I couldn't let it distract me, because that would ruin my game. It was time to compartmentalise again. After all, I had known Evie, Jaz, Mollie and Andrew for a matter of weeks, whereas my family, who had known me for my entire life, were at home waiting for me to come back.

I did feel guilty that evening (as I'd done at various times during the filming). But then I imagined what it would be like if I turned around and said, 'Look, I can't do this any more; I'm a Traitor.' I'd have to ring my dad and tell him that I got to the final, but felt too bad, so I let someone else walk away with the money. I'd have to tell him and Mum that I wouldn't be able to pay off any of their debts or repay them for the sacrifices they'd made for me. And I'd have to tell Anna that I wouldn't have a little bit of seed money for a house for the family we wanted to start.

I really liked all four people I was with in the final. We'd had the maddest moments together, like no one else will ever experience, and there was a bond there. But, at the same time, I had my head screwed on. I'd put in so much to get here, and I wasn't going to stop now. I knew what I needed to do.

What no one tells you about *The Traitors* is how little sleep you get. There are long days of filming, and the Traitors need to do more hours to capture the turret scenes. The team behind the show looked after us, giving us time off to recover from the busy schedule. But though there was plenty of opportunity to rest, everyone would come down to breakfast in the morning worn out. You see, it's the mental work that's so tiring. Every day, a great deal of information is being thrown at you, and when you go to bed, you need to process things and then, once you've done that, use what you've learned to make your plan for the next day. And for every hour a Traitor would spend plotting, a Faithful would spend the same worrying who was a Traitor and if they were about to be murdered.

I'm normally a bad sleeper, but I slept like a baby that final night. I knew I had done everything I possibly could to put myself in a great position to win.

Grandad Dave would be proud.

Waking up the next morning was the best feeling in the world. I believe confidence has played a big part in my life and where I've got to, but I still couldn't quite believe that I was on a TV show my whole family could watch on the BBC, and that I'd made it to the final. I'd done some of the most amazing things ever on the missions and played the best game I possibly could over the weeks, and now I only had this last day to enjoy. It was mad, and I was so excited to get going. I was excited for our final mission. I was excited because I had the chance to win seventy grand. I was excited because I knew that once the day was over, I would get my phone back. I was excited to speak to Anna and my family. I was excited to check the Chelsea scores and see how England had got on. I was excited not to have to lie any more. And I was excited to be Harry again.

I went down for breakfast and had my usual (coffee and biscuits) and, as I sat sipping my drink, I thought about where I was with my fellow contestants. Evie had doomed herself because she'd gone so hard for Jasmine. People had a lot of doubts about Andrew, particularly after Ross's reaction to his lie. I'm not sure Mollie ever really trusted Jaz, though she did seem to trust me, and I wasn't sure if Jaz could really convince Mollie he was a Faithful.

After breakfast, we all went outside to play croquet (they had so many games at the castle, it was great), and we saw this helicopter flying in. We figured Claudia was doing one of her crazy entrances. It's the final day, and it's Claudia Winkleman; if she wants to fly in on a helicopter, she can fly in on a helicopter. We never imagined it was for us! Despite working on helicopters in the Army, I'd never actually flown in one, so it was a crazy moment for me and the coolest thing ever to be lifted above the hills, valleys and fields where we'd been doing our challenges these last few weeks. Up there, I had another moment of reflecting on all that had happened, and about the fun mission we were about to go on that could add yet more money to a prize pot. Winning that on national television gave me the motivation to finish the game in the way I wanted to finish it.

So, we did the final mission, which was the best ever. We got to run around with a treasure map, climb through caves, abseil (which I hadn't done since Lux Nymo) and then go out to a pirate ship. I'd always wanted to be a pirate, but then I got really seasick and realised I'd probably make the worst pirate ever. Maybe I'd stick to being a pirate who just guards treasure on land. And then, after completing the mission with an extra £20,000 in the bank, we drove back to the castle to prepare for the final round table.

I got showered and went to the dressing room, where I got into my suit and waited for them to call me in. To return to where this book began, I believe the reason I sang that Frank Sinatra song was because I realised it would be easy to start overthinking everything. My mind was running at full speed. I could try to plan for every eventuality, what might happen in every single moment, who might say what to me, what I might need to say in order to survive till the end. Or I could go round in circles, wishing I'd done this or said that. Both seemed like a waste of energy. I felt as if the game had already been played. I had set everything up as well as I could.

Now, I just needed to go in there and be Harry the Traitor one last time.

Walking into that room for our final night felt weird. Everyone looked really smart and put-together, but you could tell they were churning inside, anxious yet scared to get going.

Evie opened our chat by trying to defend herself. She was really passionate, and obviously, I knew her claim to be a Faithful was true, so it was hard to hear her pleas. However, she didn't manage to sway the group, and we all voted her out. She'd got really far in the game, which I'm not sure she expected, and I think over the past couple of days she'd come to accept her fate, so she seemed OK.

After Evie left, Jaz and Mollie were scrambling to work out who might be the Traitor (or Traitors). I knew I wasn't next in the firing line—that was definitely Andrew. Ross had cast some doubts on him, and Andrew's interaction with Evie had made him seem quite guilty.

I could tell which way the wind was blowing (or so I thought), but I didn't want to be the one to kick off the accusations, because I really liked Andrew. What I failed to predict was that Andrew would go for me! I suddenly realised he was attempting to drag me down with him. (After filming had finished, I found out that he had pulled Jaz aside before the round table and told him I was the mastermind behind the whole thing.) In that moment, I had to do everything I could to stop him getting his way, including acting as shocked as I really was.

Andrew really wanted to be in the final because he knew that would help him spread awareness about the mental health causes he cared about. Taking away his chance to win the money was tough. Plus, I liked the guy. But I knew how hard he was finding it being a Traitor, and towards the end, he was really struggling. I didn't want to twist the knife, but by this point, Mollie and Jaz were too suspicious for him to get any further. So, we said goodbye. He was a warrior, and maybe I shouldn't have been surprised he fought till the end, but it was sad to see him go.

And then there were just the three of us. I thought my plan to hide the number of Traitors left had worked and that the game was going to end, but knowing what I do now about Andrew whispering in Jaz's ear, it makes sense that Jaz kept things going for one more banishment. Arguably, all he had to say (but didn't) to Mollie was that if he was a Traitor, he would never have continued the game. However, the fact that he had voted to continue must have influenced her a bit, as I could tell she suddenly wasn't sure who to believe.

We made our final cases to Mollie because we knew she had the deciding vote, and after we'd finished talking, Claudia asked us to write the name of the person we wished to banish on our slates. I knew Mollie had written mine because she wouldn't make eye contact with me. She was looking around, clearly torn. Finally, I caught her eye and told one last lie. When she asked to change her answer, I knew I could breathe. Jaz was aware of what was happening, too, and I could see his dismay.

But it was done.

When I revealed that I was a Traitor, I felt really bad for Mollie, but also so relieved. It was as if a huge burden had rolled off my shoulders. I felt I could be fully Harry again. And I hoped that one day people would be able to trust me.

Claudia told me I had won £95,000. I'm twenty-two years old and I've just won £95,000! I was shocked but also conflicted. As I'm a person with feelings, it went through my head instantly that in winning the money, I'd stopped twenty-one other people from getting it. I don't think I'd be human if I didn't feel bad for ruining those people's chances. We'd had this crazy experience together, and I'd played the game well, but did I really deserve the money more than the others?

Claudia, superwoman that she is, came to the rescue. On camera, she told me that I'd played the smartest game I could and that I'd tricked the other players into winning this money for me and my family. But off camera, she did everything she could to make me feel better about it, assuring me that it was a game; that I'd won the money and that I deserved it.

All the same, I wanted to see Mollie straight away, and it shows the kind of person she is that she wanted to see me straight away too. She reiterated what Claudia had said and then added, 'If I was in your position, I would have done the exact same thing', which helped a good deal.

I'll forever be grateful to Mollie, to Claudia and to the whole crew for not making me feel like a horrible person. I got to speak with the team at Studio Lambert about what they'd just witnessed and what we'd created. I even got to speak to the person who cast me for the show. When we talked way back then, one of the first things she told me was that she'd cast the winners of season 1 of *The Traitors*, and she asked if I remembered what I'd replied.

'Well, now you've just cast the winner of season 2.'

After saying goodbye to everyone, I left the castle. I remember not knowing what time it was (I think it was 4 or 5 in the morning, all time was lost at the round table), and the sky was pitch black. The storm had died down, but it was still raining, so my suit got a bit damp as I walked across the stone driveway and got in the taxi with one of the welfare team. As we pulled away, she handed me my phone. I opened it and called my mum and dad.

I couldn't wait to hear what they'd say.

14
LIFE AFTER

I HONESTLY COULDN'T WAIT to get home. When I had my phone back, I spoke to my mum, my dad and Anna. They all responded exactly how I thought they would. Mum was worried something was wrong (given it was the middle of the night), and once I'd assured her I was fine, she said how nice it was to hear my voice. I asked her to wake up Dad and put me on speaker phone. When they were both listening, I took a deep breath and told them I'd won. There was a moment of silence . . . then my dad began laughing—he started singing 'O happy day', like he was in a church choir! They were both so delighted. And when I got off the phone to them, I called Anna, who said multiple swear words followed by, 'Shut up, no, you didn't.' So yeah, exactly what I suspected.

Anna and I stayed up chatting the whole night. In the morning, I rang my brothers and sisters: they couldn't believe what I was telling them either. It was great to speak on the phone, but not the same as seeing them in real life, so on the train back to Slough, I was bouncing up and down in my seat. I think the people around me were a little bit puzzled, but obviously I had to keep a lid on things until the show aired in six months; by then, they would have forgotten about the strange kid who couldn't sit still.

When I got home, everyone was waiting at the door, and Anna jumped into my arms and gave me the biggest hug.

When she let go, my family all came and welcomed me back. It was the best feeling ever. Then we sat down and chatted, and I couldn't tell if my parents cared more about the money or the fact that I'd met Claudia, because they love her so much from watching *Strictly*.

It was great to celebrate and spend time with everyone again, but I only had the weekend to do so, because on Monday, as mental as it felt, I was back to work.

For the first six months after *The Traitors*, life was pretty much back to normal. I'd signed off at the Army (like handing your notice in at any other job) before I travelled up to do *The Traitors*, but I had to use my leave for the show because the Army makes you serve for a year after you've signed off. I think this is to prepare people for life as a civvy, and in that time, you can take courses in things like carpentry or bricklaying, or some other such trade. I had my qualification in Aeronautical Engineering and had already set myself up with a job on the trains in Wimbledon. I was really excited to get out into the world and start making money when my twelve months were up.

Because I was leaving, I knew the Army wasn't going to give me any of the best jobs—I was no longer being sent overseas or doing any cool training. Instead, I was told to stand on guard and sweep floors in hangars . . . amazing Scottish castles, with deer heads on the walls and suits of armour in the corridors felt a long way away. Unfortunately, the date I'd been given to leave the military was October the following year, which made no sense to me, as I'd signed off before going to Inverness in August. Even if I managed to get out earlier (and I was trying to), I'd be where I was for a while at least.

These were really confusing months. I was absolutely buzzing after having what I think was the best moment of my life. I longed to share it with the world, yet I could only tell my closest loved ones. When I'd gone back to the Army, I was grinning from ear to ear, but after three or four weeks, that smile faded. I was surrounded by people who had no idea what I'd achieved—and I was sweeping floors.

I also started to worry about what the public might think of me. The final of the first season was viewed by almost five million people, and while I knew the drama of season two would make it amazing to watch, there was no guarantee our audience would get to that level. But whatever number we reached, how would they respond to what happened? Would the whole nation hate me? I'd just ruined twenty-one other people's chances of winning that money, and it wasn't like I'd won it by hunting down Traitors: I'd murdered these people and traitored my way to the top.

It was time to compartmentalise again. I locked those thoughts away and returned to boxing and football and the things I've always enjoyed in my life. *The Traitors*, season 2, would come round soon enough.

At the beginning of 2024, I'd just torn my ACL at footie and could barely walk, so I was off on medical leave from the Army and wearing a massive boot to help my ligaments repair. This was kind of great timing, because I had no regular leave left and (as it turned out), I needed the time off.

On the 2nd of January (the show would go out on the BBC on the 3rd), the crew and contestants were invited to an opening party, where we'd all watch the first episode together. It was good to see the others after such a long time apart; it felt like being back in the game. Of course, I couldn't tell anyone what had happened because no one could know until the final aired.

After we sat down in the theatre, Claudia came out on stage and did a little introduction, which was brilliant. What wasn't brilliant was seeing myself on screen. I always find myself the biggest ick—I can't even listen to my own voice notes—so when I saw myself up there, I was pretty embarrassed. The other contestants were really excited, though. Whenever a new person was introduced, everyone cheered, and as the episode finished, there was a massive round of applause.

Much more fun for me was watching the show with my family. When the first three episodes were released on iPlayer, we crammed as many people as we could into our living room. No one could stop laughing. Every time I did or said something, they'd be like 'That's the exact same stupid stuff you say at home', or 'How have they not clocked onto you yet?' Obviously, only my parents, my brothers and sisters and Anna knew I'd won, and it was entertaining seeing the others watch events unfold. They had no idea what was about to happen, and I was sitting there thinking, 'Just you wait.'

The next weeks were crazy. The first three episodes were available to view on iPlayer on Friday, and all weekend, I had random people coming up to me in the street, asking me what was going to happen. Friends were texting me, and journalists were asking for interviews. I made my Instagram public and gained about 50,000 followers. It felt strange to know that if I posted a story, 50,000 people might see it. The buzz would die down on Monday and Tuesday, but when a new episode came out on Wednesday, the madness returned. People in my area were renting out pubs and stuff to watch, but as I hadn't received my prize money yet, I didn't really have the funds for that. Plus, I just wanted to sit at home and watch the show with my family.

In the next few weeks, in response to messages from agents, I had about sixteen different meetings with talent agencies. I was so grateful to have Anna: she and her family were really helpful and, as the show progressed, they told me they thought I could actually make being a public figure into my job. I was a Traitor, but people in the UK appeared to love me, and I seemed to be coming out of the show really well. Even now, when I'm out with Paul, someone will often walk up and tell us that they loved me and wanted me to win, before turning to Paul and saying they hated him. Paul just laughs and says, 'You know, he was ten times worse than me!' I couldn't be more grateful for that response from the public, partly because it's funny and partly because it shows that people saw *The Traitors* like I did, as a game. Normally, everyone roots for the good guys, and the Faithfuls are the good guys, so it's a nice feeling when you're actually the bad guy and you hear that people still wanted you to go all the way, just because of the game you were playing. There'll always be haters, but I'm still happy, to this day, that most people don't judge me for trying to win.

However, at the time, I didn't really have that perspective. I was shocked that people in the entertainment industry felt I could build on what I'd done. I loved the idea of making my family proud by being on TV more, and it was great to hear from friends about the show, but I was happy just to take the money and go and work on the trains. I believe, though, that what brilliant TV does is bring joy to people. And they're so happy you gave that, that they grow to have fond memories of you.

I remember one day I was putting my suitcase in the back of an Uber, ready to go to London, when the driver came running around. He was moving so fast, I thought he was going to try and nick my suitcase or something, but he just wanted to get a selfie. I was like, 'Of course', and after we'd taken it and he'd sent it to his family WhatsApp, we got into the car and chatted the whole way. He told me that his dad is still alive and his sons are all different ages—an adult of twenty, a teenager of thirteen and a child of five—and that *The Traitors* was the only thing that had brought all the generations of his family together. They'd sit on the sofa every Friday night, order a takeaway and watch all three episodes in one go. And he told me that everyone was rooting for me because I was just a kid from Slough who had come from nothing (or, at least, next to nothing, I know I'm lucky to have such a great community), and that it had inspired his sons to go on and do what they wanted to do.

That was the moment I seriously considered giving this a shot. I've always wanted to help others, and I thought to myself, if a kid who grew up in a council house can get on well, it shows people you can do anything you set your mind to, I'll take the next step. And I figured if everything suddenly came to an end, I'd still be happy, because I'd given it my all.

I'm not sure I realised quite how big the whole thing would get.

The four weeks of the show airing passed by in a flash, with everyone getting more and more excited that I was making it through each round. Then, for the final episode, the production company invited us to an even bigger screening in a theatre in London. We all got to bring someone, so naturally Anna accompanied me. I had her on one side of me and Paul on the other, as we sat down in front of these huge red curtains. I hadn't told Paul what had happened in the final, but when we met at that event, he leaned over and whispered, 'I know you've won the show.' Playing dumb, I was like, 'What do you mean?' and he just said, 'When I got voted out, I knew you'd go on and win. I don't want to know how, though; I want to watch it like everyone else.' All I could do was laugh nervously.

Anyway, as before, Claudia appeared on stage and said something amazing (because she is amazing), and after she'd finished, the curtains opened, the lights dimmed, and the final episode was projected on the screen.

Obviously, I knew what happened, but I still thought it was completely gripping. I was on the edge of my seat the whole time wondering, How does this guy make it out of that? Is he actually going to get away with everything? There was a point when I wondered if I did actually win. Maybe I'd dreamed it or something, and the dream was all about to unravel in front of my eyes. But as the episode went on, things started to come together again in my head . . . suddenly, I could remember everything happening, just as if I was there. The helicopter, the mission, the five of us at the round table.

This episode was new to everyone else, though. It felt weird that there were 200 to 300 people in the room, and I was one of only a handful who knew what was about to happen. When Mollie wrote my name down on the board, everyone cheered, which was probably to be expected with so many Faithfuls in the room. As I said, people want the good guys to win. Then I began to worry again about what everyone was going to think of what happened next. When Mollie then wiped off my name and wrote down Jaz's, everyone went very quiet, except for Paul, who said, 'Go on Harry!' The big reveal took place, and I watched myself walk out of the castle with Claudia. The whole theatre heard me shout, 'I'm the best Traitor in the world!'

The credits rolled, and I felt as if I'd won an Oscar, but it was also a really awkward moment. Then, all of a sudden, everyone rose up from their seats and began clapping and cheering. People were turning to me and patting me on the back. I was the only person sitting down—even Anna was on her feet, looking quite proud. The standing ovation went on for about five minutes, and as I realised what was happening, I felt a weight lift off my shoulders. For the past six months, I hadn't been able to shake a feeling of guilt. Even after Claudia told me I'd played a brilliant game and deserved the money. Even after I went home to my family and they told me how well I'd done. Even after the show started to air and people seemed to be responding well to the way I was playing the game. Even after all that, I was still worried about what everyone was going to think of me. But in that moment, the guilt lifted, the worry went away, and I realised that maybe it was going to be OK.

After the viewing, we all went to the bar and, because this was the night the final was being shown on the BBC, you could literally see *The Traitors* playing on the screens around the bar.

The moment the episode was over, my phone started buzzing. I was getting texts and calls from everyone I knew, and my Instagram following almost instantly went up to 170,000. I thought, this must be what it's like when an influencer has a viral moment. I FaceTimed home, and my granny was crying. My mum said she thought it was one of the best things she'd ever seen on TV.

The next week was wild. I did loads of radio, and I remember being in a taxi on the way to appearing on *This Morning* with Rylan, when Dad messaged me saying, 'Check your digits'. I thought that was pretty weird, as I only ever get thumbs up emojis from my dad, so I ignored him. But then he messaged again in all caps saying, 'CHECK YOUR ONLINE BANKING', and I saw that the prize money had been deposited in one big payment. It was the maddest thing, and it probably made my chat on *This Morning* quite fun to watch.

When I went on these shows, I wasn't wearing my boot as I didn't want the interview to just be about my footie injury. But that meant I got some suspicious messages from people in the Army, wondering if I was actually injured. Shortly after the final episode of *The Traitors,* I was called into the office of my new CO (Commanding Officer). I was nervous because the last time I'd spoken to the Army about the show was when I'd told them I was going on it, and they'd said they wanted nothing to do with it, given the nature of it was about lying. So, this morning, when I walked in with my beret on and my whole uniform nice and crisp, I really had no idea what to expect.

The second the door closed, I was told to sit down and take my beret off. Unlike my previous CO, who hated the idea of the show, it turned out my new one had not only watched *The Traitors* but loved it. He offered me a genuine thank you for bringing so much enjoyment and entertainment to his family. In addition, he understood that I'd been presented with a big opportunity, and he said the Army wasn't going to stop me from grabbing it . . . This man would turn out to be my guardian angel.

That Sunday, I got a call from camp saying I needed to come back and get my stuff, because my last day in the military was tomorrow. Normally, you'd have months to pack up and they'd throw you a leaving party, but I didn't even have a chance to go to the pub with Josh and my best mates. I gave my uniform in, signed my rifle back into the armoury and went to the office, where they snapped my Army card right in front of me.

My life was so hectic at that point that I didn't have time to think about anything. But after seven years in the military, doing a job that I'd dreamed of and loved, I was no longer a soldier.

I would pay heavily for not giving myself time to work through all the emotions involved in coming to terms with that.

I began to make full use of my freedom and went to as many events and interviews as possible: if someone sent me an invite, I accepted. One of the coolest that arrived was from the BAFTAs. Paul and I went together, both in full tux, both looking sharp, and at one point, Ant and Dec came up to us and told us they were big fans, which was surreal. The BAFTAs were fantastic, as were all these swanky events. There was a constant supply of free booze and amazing food, and before your glass was empty, someone would hand you another; before you could get hungry, a waiter would come round with a tray of delicious food. And when you're chatting to cool industry people or bumping into famous ones you never thought you'd meet, you don't want to leave. I sometimes couldn't believe what my life had become.

One of the craziest moments was when I went to Manchester to do *BBC Breakfast*. Anna came with me as support, and we had a coffee in the green room before I was taken off to talk about *The Traitors*. When I returned, she was having a chat with Gary Neville . . . not my team (he's a Manchester United man), but I let that go because he's still an absolute footballing legend. Gary was going on the show to talk about a company he'd invested in, but as that wasn't until a bit later, we had a chance to talk. At the time, I still didn't have management or an agent, partly because they all presented me with massive 200-page contracts to check, and even if I hadn't had dyslexia, I wouldn't have known what I was looking for. I told Gary that I didn't want to fall into one of those traps you hear about, where all your money's taken off you, and he said he understood.

Then someone told him it was his turn on the sofa, and he asked them to hold on a minute before turning to me and saying, 'Harry, can we get a picture?' I was literally like 'What are you on about? You're Gary Neville—I should be getting a picture with you!' But he told me his daughter loved me and would really appreciate it. Then he said, 'Give me your phone, actually', and he put his number in. He told me to send him a message and that he'd help sort my contract stuff out. I thought he was just being nice, but when he went on *BBC Breakfast*, he told the presenters what he'd just done, so I figured he must be serious.

As I mentioned earlier, I'd met with sixteen different agents. Most seemed to be selling a dream: whatever you said you wanted to do, they said they could make it happen. However, Alex Segal at InterTalent was different. He had a one-year, five-year and ten-year plan for me, which was exactly the kind of longevity I was looking for. I was sold. And then the first thing I did when I decided I wanted to go with InterTalent was to message Gary Neville. It still feels weird even saying that.

Gary and his lawyer went through every line of my contract and negotiated the best deal ever. Not only that, Gary paid for it all and hasn't asked me for a penny since. I'll forever be grateful to him for his help and to Alex and the team at InterTalent for taking a risk on me.

Once I'd signed with the agency, life got even crazier. Alex and I were working together to boost my profile, and within the space of eighteen months, I did thirty-two pieces of TV. It does feel a little mad to say that now. There was *The One Show*, *The Weakest Link* and *Celebrity Antiques Roadshow* all in the same year, as well as some great presenting opportunities.

I think everyone's got an engine, and that engine will have a certain amount of capacity. I was loving everything so much that I was going full throttle. As well as all the TV and presenting jobs, there seemed to be an event every night in London. I was constantly thinking that now could be my last chance to enjoy this stuff, and that I'd be back at work on the trains the following week. So, I made the most of it, and because of that, I was drinking all the time. As I said, you finish one drink, another's in your hand, and you never have to pay for a single thing. Also, I remembered from my Army days that the best way to get over a hangover was to start drinking again, so if I needed to go to another event on a day when I was feeling rough, rather than take it easy, that's what I'd do.

I got into a loop of doing this every night and failed to realise I was losing myself in the process. With all the drinking, all the food, and seemingly no chance to do any fitness (as I was so busy), I was also putting on weight. It was like my first six months in the Army all over again, only this time I justified things by telling myself that I should be enjoying the ride.

Then Alex told me they'd had an offer from *Celebrity SAS*.

Straight away, I knew it was a bad idea for me to do that show. I love watching it, but at the time, I weighed over 100 kilos, and as we had only two weeks' notice, I'd have to go on at the heaviest I'd ever been. (It would have been better to delay my participation, but the offer might not be there in a year's time.) Plus, these guys were ex-SAS soldiers, and I knew they'd expect someone who'd been in the military to be able to do all the fitness stuff.

I was aware that I was lost physically, but I didn't realise quite how lost I was mentally. All I'd done since I'd left the Army was work. I hadn't given myself a chance to process my emotions about leaving the military, and now I was about to go back into that environment, quite unprepared.

Also, despite having worked in the entertainment industry for a year, I didn't feel settled there either. The people I was going to be with on *Celebrity SAS* had been famous for years or even decades, and the second I stepped into the camp with them, I already felt like an imposter. I mean, they'd been at the top for years and grown comfortable with fame; I was still living at my parents' house and driving my Vauxhall Corsa around Slough! In addition, I was the youngest, and I knew that would count against me in the fitness trials, and that I'd be judged more harshly for not meeting the required standard.

It was a recipe for disaster. However, I figured that, as in the Army, if I made mistakes, I could correct them and push on. In the Army, they don't want you to fail. They push you to your limits, but they also tell you what you're doing wrong, and I love this: it's an opportunity for self-improvement, and I always want to be getting better. I loved—and am proud to have been—a part of the military. But wanting so much not to let the Army down added extra pressure that I wasn't mentally ready for.

Celebrity SAS went about as badly as I expected.

When I got home, I felt as if I was back in the deep, dark hole I'd experienced towards the end of my Army career.

I was still drinking all the time. My weight had gone up to 106 kilos, and I had absolutely no confidence left. Because of this, Anna and I were having a really tough time.

I've always said that Anna and I have had one of the hardest relationships because every time we're getting settled, something bad happens. I was going out to all these events, some of which Anna was invited to and some of which she wasn't. Around this time, she was settling into the idea of having a quieter life out of the limelight anyway, so sometimes even when she was invited, she wouldn't come.

When I went out in the evening on my own, I'd often be too drunk to message her back; during the day, I'd be too busy working to respond to her, and when I saw her in the evenings, I just wasn't myself. I'd have used up so much energy by then trying to be happy clappy Harry (because I felt so miserable), that when I got home, all I wanted to do was play *Call of Duty* and go to bed.

When your relationship is in the public eye, people tend only to see the good side of it and think you have it really easy. But there are always those who want to see you fail, and are even willing you to do so. Some in the industry were spreading rumours that weren't true, and a lot of the time, Anna or I or both of us were getting messages to test the strength of our relationship. The timing was absolutely terrible, given what was going on with me. I think it's hard to love someone who doesn't love themselves, and as I was battling my demons, I really wasn't in a good place. You can't expect someone to wait around forever, and it had been over a year since I'd really felt good about myself.

I was in a dark place again, with a whole new set of problems that I felt unable to handle. Thankfully, this time I knew what I needed to do. I began leaning on the people around me, particularly my dad, my mum and Alex, who was a really strong support and helped me understand that in this world there are ups and downs, but that I had a lot going for me. Dad, similarly, made me realise that perhaps things weren't as bad as I was making out. But, of course, it was my mum who really helped. She gave me the advice she had given me those years before, and which had proved so useful.

So, I began praying again. I really needed guidance and a path forward, and I remember what I prayed for clearly, because it was what I said every time I sat down: 'God, you know I love you. If I forget you, don't forget me. Please just give me a sign.'

And that was when I got a call from Alex.

'Harry, are you religious?'

15
PILGRIMAGE

MY MUM ALWAYS SAYS that God tests his toughest soldiers. It's one of my favourite quotes because it assures me that God is there when I'm in the middle of a challenging time, and that I'm strong enough to get through any ordeal. Sometimes it feels crazy that I'm only twenty-four and have already been tested so much in my life, but then I'll reflect on how I'll no doubt be tested more, and that whatever I have to endure, it's part of a plan.

Around and after *The Traitors*, my connection to religion went foggy, simply because I wasn't making time for it. Then Alex got that call. It was for a BBC show called *Pilgrimage*, in which (as I explained earlier) celebrities walk a historic pilgrimage route and discuss their faith. For the seventh season of the show, the journey would be through the Austrian and Swiss Alps, and they wanted me to join. I had asked for a sign, and it felt as if accepting this offer would help give me a clearer vision of what I was to do in my life. I had no idea who the other people on the pilgrimage were going to be, but the trip sounded incredible. I had prayed, and this appeared to be an answer.

I told Alex, 'Yes.'

Given my recent TV experience (on *Celebrity SAS*), I was understandably nervous. Actually, I was petrified. What if I didn't get on with any of the others? The pilgrimage was two weeks of walking for hours and hours every day, and as we were all staying at the same accommodation overnight, there would be plenty of evenings together too.

You don't meet your fellow pilgrims before the show, so the film crew can catch your first reactions on camera. My celebrity imposter syndrome was kicking in as I walked up the big hill to meet everyone. It was quite a warm day, and as I was carrying a large bag, I was pretty sweaty by the time I reached the top. My travelling companions might be wondering who on earth this strange, perspiring outsider was. However, it turned out I had nothing to worry about. The second I got there, everyone was so friendly that my concerns just melted away.

The only person I instantly recognised was Jeff Brazier. I've seen him on TV loads, and also I think my mum fancies him a little bit, which makes him quite memorable. (I'm pretty sure every mum fancies Jeff Brazier; he's one of those guys.) But he didn't know me, because he hadn't watched *The Traitors*. The only people who had seen the show were Helen (Lederer, the comedian) and Jay (McGuiness, from The Wanted), which was perfect (in that there were only these two), because if you had seen me in that, you'd never trust a word I said, and I already liked these people and wanted them to like me.

You could tell almost straight away that everyone in the group was going to contribute something different, including in terms of faith. For anyone who hasn't yet had the chance to watch the series (and if not, definitely go to iPlayer to catch up), I was on pilgrimage with: Helen, who was exploring her mixed Jewish and Protestant heritage; Jay, who identified as agnostic and wanted to investigate that more and see whether he might actually be an atheist; Nelafur Hedayat, a journalist and broadcaster, who is Muslim; Stefanie Reid, a paralympic athlete, who has a strong Christian faith; Daliso Chaponda, a comedian who was veering towards the Baha'i faith; and my man Jeff, who didn't identify with one religion but is very spiritual.

As preparation for *Pilgrimage*, I'd decided to take a deep dive into all the major religions. In the process of doing so, I began to ask myself why I was a Roman Catholic. Was it just because I was born into a Roman Catholic family and my mum took me to church? I didn't want to go in there and give the impression I thought my faith was truer than anyone else's. I wanted to hear from the others, learn from them, and hopefully understand my own relationship with religion more.

Also, I wanted to show that you can be young and still have faith. I've always believed that religion is about your own journey, and that what you're personally going through is more relevant than your age or circumstances in life.

I guess I wanted to prove that to myself, too.

Inzing, where we gathered that first morning, is an amazing little village, surrounded by snow-capped mountains. I felt as if we were in a movie, it was so picturesque. We had twelve days of hiking ahead, and I'd have liked to have been in better shape, but I knew after taking only a few steps that going on *Pilgrimage* was a great decision.

I set off with Helen, and we bonded straight away. Soon, I began calling her my queen, and she eventually became the queen of the Three Musketeers (which was me, Helen and Jay). She is one of the funniest people I've ever met, so quick-witted, and from the very first moment, she was brilliant to talk to. She asked me loads of questions—about *The Traitors* and about my religion, and she told me about hers. She seemed quite confused, because her family were Jewish, but in the light of the historic atrocities against Jews, they'd sort of converted away from Judaism to Christianity. I think she was concerned about not wholly following one religion or the other, but I told her that it was fine not to feel fully one thing. Everyone's relationship to their faith is different, and she did find great comfort in praying to God. We spoke about that a lot.

We also talked about being on TV. I was obviously dealing with some complicated feelings, and she's been on TV for over fifty years, so the wisdom she imparted was incredibly useful. She told me that ultimately I was going to be fine, and that was the nicest thing ever to hear, especially from a legend like Helen. I think we both learnt a lot in that first chat, and we kept talking throughout the entire two weeks. She was fantastic to be around, and when we've met up since, she still makes me laugh so much.

The others in the group seemed to be making connections, too. We mingled really well together and chatted constantly as we walked through those unbelievable landscapes. So many times, we'd have to stop and take a moment to look around, because we'd been so deep in conversation that we'd forgotten to notice the green hills, rolling fields, calm forests, amazing little villages on the side of blue lakes . . . and always, those huge mountains in the background. I'm sure the sounds of nature would have been great to listen to, but we had too much to learn from one another, so the chats took over.

The other person I spoke to about the industry was Jeff, who had fifteen or twenty years' experience by this stage. When I told him my worries—my constant concern that work would dry up, and how I feared *Pilgrimage* might be the last thing I was invited to do—he reassured me. He's into meditation and has this very calming presence, and I think he saw a lot of himself as a younger man in me, so he could really connect with what I was feeling. Being in an industry where you don't know whether or not you're working the next day is scary, and it wasn't something I could easily talk about with my family. They'd all had nine-to-five (or at least salaried) jobs all their lives. But Jeff cheered me by pointing out that I wouldn't be in the position I was in if people didn't want me there. After all, you've got this far reading my book, and I'm not sure you'd have kept going if you weren't enjoying it at some level! I'm grateful to anyone who supports me enough to help me in my career.

Jeff did make me see, though, that there will always be ups and downs. He's had a hard life, and given everything that's happened to him, I'm not surprised he may not feel as if God is in his life. However, he believes in energy and he believes in meditation, and his spirituality and confidence in a higher power have helped him weather the storm, which I think is a great lesson for everyone, whether you have faith or not.

As well as being a great place to learn and grow, the pilgrimage was also just really fun. For a start, I got to share a bed with

Jeff Brazier (I know, living the dream), and I was so excited to spoon with him. That was a few days in, though, once Jeff and I had become better acquainted.

On the first day of the trip, we got to meet a monk, and then later on, we met a nun. Both were such cool experiences. I can't even remember to pray every day, and these were people who devoted their whole lives to their faith. Yet, I got to see them as just normal people (and I hugged them both—I hugged everyone on that trip!) During his life, Pope Francis said that he was no better than anyone else; that he was no closer to God than anyone else; that he was just a teacher. I like that about my religion, and it was great to meet these men and women, who are at the top of any scale in terms of devotion, and to find they are just people, dedicating themselves wholeheartedly to serving God in the world.

The monastery the monk belonged to brewed beer, which we were invited to sample. I'm not going to lie: to me, it tasted like any normal beer, and as with any normal beer, I had a few. Jay and I sat up quite late chatting over drinks, which is how we became so close so quickly.

Jay was in a really interesting place, not only with his faith, but in his life. I sensed he was quite confused, still grieving the loss of his bandmate, and not sure where he belonged or what he belonged to. I could relate to this, as when bad stuff happened to me, I really questioned if there was a God. I wanted to help shoulder some of the burden he was carrying, so I told him everything I'd gone through towards the end of my Army career—how I managed to come out the other side of that, and about the place I was in now. Sometimes, all it takes is to hear something you've never thought about before for something to click in your mind and move you out of wherever you are. I hoped our chats together were helping a little bit.

Jay and I became really close and enjoyed so many things together on that trip. For Helen's birthday, we arranged a little party at a place called The Pilgrim Post, which was a spa near a cattle farm. Naturally, the cattle set off my allergies, so I spent the whole day and evening sneezing, and really wasn't looking forward to trying to sleep that night. Then, at 2 a.m., the farm cockerel started crowing and didn't stop until 5 a.m. I was in bits, and kept getting up and asking when it was going to shut up, but Jay was laughing his head off.

In the morning, I desperately needed to wake up, so I asked him if he wanted to go and have a bath, given we were at a spa. The bath turned out to be more of a wooden barrel that you sat in, and it had a bag of warm water set above it. You used a hose attached to the bag to wash, but because there was only one bag, Jay and I had to share, and as we were both in the barrel together, neither of us had enough elbow space to wash ourselves, so we were basically hosing each other with this trickle of warm water. Given it was so early in the morning (thanks to the cockerel), it was freezing, and Jay and I were fighting each other for a hose that barely had enough water in it for one person, let alone two. Then the hostess of the spa, who didn't speak a word of English, came over and kindly held it over us. So, there we were, two grown men, in a bath/barrel, getting hosed down by a woman who could only say 'Hello' in English, in the magnificent surroundings of the Swiss Alps. It was the funniest thing ever, and I'm so glad they put it in the show.

For better or worse, once again, I just couldn't believe this was my life.

Jay and I had a similar sense of humour, but in terms of belief, I was closest to Stef, or, as I came to call her, The Angel Stef.

She was a Christian and seemed to know literally everything about the Bible and the Scriptures. If anyone ever had a question about religion, they would ask her, and to me, she was like a teacher. I wanted to learn as much from her as possible in our time together.

Stef was generous enough to share the story of what happened to her, and I think we all came to see how her experiences, her outlook and her faith were linked. It was amazing to witness, and I really admired her approach to life and how she kept herself together. I don't think I ever saw her get upset or angry, or even frown. She radiated contentment, and when you looked at her, you thought, the world is a much happier place with Stef in it.

It was fascinating being with Stef and at the same time with Nelafur, who seemed to be so conflicted about her religion. She'd had a really hard life, and I think that was why she connected so well with Jeff, but I saw her become closer to Stef as well. It's eye-opening when you're struggling with your faith to meet Stef, as she's so dedicated to hers, and I think Nelafur found some insight in that.

When I spoke to Nelafur, I thought I could feel her pain. She's a fantastic journalist and an incredibly hard worker, and I think she was putting that same effort into trying to solve her conflict over her faith. I personally think faith can be the easiest thing ever, but I do understand that we all have different experiences. The group was open-minded, with no one forcing their beliefs on anyone else. Even if I couldn't quite vibe with someone's view, we'd still have a fascinating conversation. Nelafur and I were at such different places, yet our talks were always interesting.

As we continued journeying through the Swiss Alps, I began to understand the power of community, particularly when we're struggling, and how important it was to lean on those around you—and just to talk.

Daliso was the coolest person to chat to because he was interested in every religion. Also, he knew so much: speaking to him really helped me understand why I'm Roman Catholic. He has been to or lived in around 200 countries, and whenever he goes to a new place, he'll attend the nearest place of worship—whether a church, a mosque or a synagogue. He was like a religious butterfly, and that was such a breath of fresh air. The reason he'd decided to explore the Baha'i faith in particular was because, as he described it, they believe that all faiths are just different paths on a quest for truth.

It was great to get an insight into what other faiths believed, because, as I mentioned, that clarified for me what drew me to mine. As we got closer to the end of our journey, I felt my understanding had deepened. Daliso helped me more than I think he'll ever know.

I have always felt that God puts me in the place in my life that I need to be; I was beginning to realise that he draws others there too. I needed not only Daliso, but the whole group on that trip, in different ways and for different reasons. They were there for me and answered all my weird questions, and for that, I'll be forever grateful.

Walking into Einsieldeln Abbey on the final day felt like coming home. After two weeks on the road with my fellow pilgrims, it was great to arrive at our destination (my feet were killing me!), and the abbey itself is incredible—with amazing high ceilings and beautiful architecture.

As I sat down in a pew, I reflected on everything I'd learned on my own personal journey. Before I set off, I wanted to discover more about my faith, about why I am Roman Catholic. I'd come to understand that the Roman Catholic faith resonates most with me because of the lessons it teaches. It's hard to boil this down, but I see a great deal about kindness and helping people, and I want my life to revolve around these things. In that sense, the pilgrimage hadn't changed my faith but strengthened it.

Putting my hands together in the abbey, I thought about how grateful I was to be in this exact place in my life right now. God had gifted me this journey, and he had shown me that even in my darkest moments, there was light. I hadn't gone on *Pilgrimage* for the fame or the money, but because God knew it was what I needed.

And I thought about how that might actually help a few people. I hope people watch the show and find something that speaks to them in it. A bit like this book.

When I started writing, I wanted people to get a deeper sense of who I am, where I come from and what's happened to me in my life. I've tried to make sure the book is as personal as possible. It's been a brilliant thing to work on, and I'm not only grateful for the opportunity to produce it, but I'm grateful to you for having read it (all the way to the end!)

I should mention that I always get a lot out of hearing other people's stories, and I hope that hearing mine has offered you something—whether that's an escape from reality, an insight into what other people go through, or some lesson that helps motivate you to go on and do what you really want to. And if you're struggling or just generally having a tough time, I want to say that tomorrow is a new day and there's a chance that everything will get better. If you're at your worst, know that your best is yet to come. Do whatever you feel like you need to in order to remind yourself of all the good you have at your fingertips: start walking, listen to music, pray if that works for you, speak to someone if it doesn't, think about everything in your life that is going well and trust that even if it's not, better things are coming. Have faith in that.

There are a lot of bad things happening in the world these days, and it's so easy to be negative, but if this book has helped bring even a little bit of positivity and joy into your life, then I'm happy.

Afterword

Afterword

I didn't want to leave you hanging on a few things, given you've come this far, so here's a little afterword.

Pilgrimage saved me mentally, and really got me out of that hole I was in after *The Traitors*. I felt as if I started to find myself again, but I knew I still had some things to do. I very much needed to get back to myself physically and regain the confidence I'd had before. And like she always has done, Anna was there to help me pick up the pieces.

As soon as I got home from Switzerland, Anna told me we were going to First Class Boot Camp, a fitness retreat. Anna's always been so much more advanced than me, always so much more mature, and basically, she hits stages and has realisations quicker than I do. (Personally, I think it's the same with every woman and man, to be honest.) Anna had really been into her fitness for about six months, but I didn't understand how I could get involved. She had to force me, but eventually we went on this week-long fitness camp together. I think she knew I wasn't going to want to talk about anything (I'm not much of a talker), so she put action over words.

We both fell in love with the retreat. It was run by a guy called Tom Brown and his fiancé Sophie, and now they're two of the most important people in my life. Tom's my PT and he's taught me so much about discipline and motivation (and also how often I can eat pizza and not feel bad about it). The retreat was like a mini pilgrimage for my body; it changed my entire view on life, my motivation and my sense of balance. I focused less on work and started reminding myself of what the people around me had been saying—which was that I was going to be OK. Suddenly, I had energy to give to my family and friends, and I began to focus on the people who were important to me again. After I'd lost some weight, I started to get my confidence back, too. All of this helped my relationship.

I think that anyone who tells you their relationship is perfect is the biggest liar, and I said before I did this book that we weren't going to put any lies in it. Mine and Anna's relationship is far from perfect. We've been through some tough times, but I think what makes ours a good relationship or a relationship that works is that (like I've seen my parents doing), we both put everything into it, and if one of us is struggling, we help the other. That's what Anna's done. She loves me for being me, not for being Harry from *The Traitors* or having won that money. She's believed in me, stuck by me and made the effort when it was beyond me. We're stronger than ever, and I'm so grateful to her for that.

Now we go on runs together, and when we do, it's always the best part of my day. What more could I ask for? My prayers have been answered.

Acknowledgements

I have so many people to thank, this might take a while. But I'll start with one of the easiest ones: you, the reader. You're here because you've come out and read this book, and you've read all the way to the end (unless you've skipped) because you care enough to follow my journey. I'm really appreciative of anyone who supports me, and you have done just that with this book, so thank you so, so much. I genuinely wouldn't be here, in this great place in my career and in my life, without you.

Next is the team that helped me put the book together. If you thought I wrote this book, then thank you for thinking that, but, as you probably know by now, I'm dyslexic and not talented enough to write a book, so a special shout-out goes to my ghostwriter, Oli Holden-Rea. After chatting to me and listening to me ramble, he turned it all into a book, making it into a great story and capturing everything I wanted to say perfectly (which is hard to do, given how I talk). I love everything that's been written and the book we've produced together. It would not have been possible if it weren't for him, and I'll always be grateful for that.

Also, a huge thank you to Oscar Janson-Smith, my literary agent, who did the deal and who helped me realise my dreams of becoming a published author. What a guy. And a huge thank you to Alison Barr, who decided to publish the book and has done that brilliantly. She's the nicest person ever and has been really, really patient with me when it comes to edits, so I appreciate everything she has done and continues to do for the book. What a woman.

Of all the team behind me, the biggest thank you goes to Alex Segal, my manager at InterTalent. He likes to say he's the brother that I never had, and I do think of him now as family. He's protected me and guided me through this crazy industry that I didn't even know existed before I'd gone on *The Traitors*, and he's been there every step of the way. If I'm stressing out or worried about anything, I know I can call him and he'll be there for me. As I've said, every rock needs a rock, and he's been that for me in this industry. I'm not sure he realises how much he's helped me and my family.

Following on from Alex, a special mention has to go to the team at InterTalent: Georgia Lloyd-Roberts, Zoe Brookes, Kate Skeffington and Esme Coyne, who I love working so closely with, as well as Professor Jonathan Shalit OBE for even just taking a chance on a kid who didn't know what he wanted to be. It was probably pretty scary hiring a 23-year-old kid from the Army who'd only been on one TV show, had never been a celebrity and had never had any media training. I'm a risk-taker, and luckily, they are too, and I couldn't be more grateful to them for giving me a shot.

As you can tell, I've got a huge team behind me and Rozzie Inge, my PR Manager, is a star of that team. She makes sure I don't do anything too horrendous to my image and looks after me in ways I probably don't even know. Thank you, Rozzie. And a big thank you to Laura Sinclair at Dawbell as well.

Speaking of huge teams, I'd like to thank all the contestants from not just season 2, but all the seasons of *The Traitors*. We've been through something no one else has, and I think that's given us a bond that no one will ever understand, and that's really special. We created such a captivating, entertaining TV show together, which I'll forever be proud of.

But, of all the people I was on the show with, I'd especially like to thank Paul. Paul has always been by my side and has always been my outlet to laugh and not be mature at all in any given situation. We can just have a laugh together, and whenever we do, it takes me out of whatever reality I'm in for a minute and puts me back in that castle, where all we ever did was make jokes out of nothing. I think he doesn't realise how much that means to me, to be able to let off steam with him whenever he comes down to London to film a podcast. It's something I never knew I needed in my life, and I couldn't be luckier to be on that show and meet someone like him. Thanks, man.

Obviously, I'd like the thank the whole team at the BBC and Studio Lambert. I got so lucky, because if Studio Lambert and the BBC hadn't taken a chance on me, I would never have been a Traitor in season 2, and I'd probably still be in the Army, lying in a ditch somewhere getting rained on, sort of hating life. A special mention to Syeda Irtizaali, Neil McCallum, Kate Phillips, Sarah Fay and David Gordon, and everyone who worked on that amazing show. Plus, Lou Plank and Susan Collins for their hard work and help after the show aired.

And, of course, Claudia. Claudia is, like, the ultimate queen. Each day, while I'm in this industry, she is someone that I look up to as an idol. Her confidence and the natural ability she has to entertain everyone are something I admire so much. She is a major part of what makes *The Traitors* so brilliant. Plus, she's one of the reasons I am where I am today, because if she hadn't chosen me to be a Traitor, I would have been a Faithful and, to be honest, probably would have gone straight away. I can never thank her enough for giving me the opportunity to be a Traitor. I hope that everything I carry on and continue to do makes her proud, because she's had a big part to play in that.

Speaking of influential people, I'm so grateful to Gary Neville. He came into my life at the exact moment I needed him and sorted out my whole contract, word by word, for two weeks. He got me the best deal ever and has never asked for anything in return. He didn't even know me as a person, and still decided to spend his time helping me out, and it just shows how nice a man he is and how much he actually does care. Without his help, I wouldn't be in the position I am today.

Thank you, also, to CTVC, the production company that made *Pilgrimage* and who took a risk to have me on that show. I'm not sure they realise how grateful I am for that, as it was what I needed in my life and it hasn't just strengthened my faith, it's strengthened me as a person and given me the balance, confidence and really everything I need to carry on with what I'm doing. Special mention to Caroline Matthews, Karen Emsley, Tom Allright, Toni Williamson and David Allberry for casting me and the commissioner at the BBC, Daisy Scalchi. The people behind the scenes are genuinely the superheroes of these programmes, and I appreciate everything they have done and continue to do.

But the people in front of the camera also need to be thanked. A shout-out to my fellow pilgrims, who all deserve a thank you: Jeff, Helen, Jay, Daliso, Stef and Nelafur. They were so welcoming as a group, I loved our chats, and they each, in their own way, gave me the confidence to carry on.

I think all they had to do was tell me I was going to be fine, but they did so much more than that, and I don't think they realise how much that meant to me. Thank you, all.

Onto the people who know me personally. Starting with Paul and the Winstanley family. Paul, his wife Zoe and his son Harry are close friends to my family, and they've given us some of the best times we've ever had in our lives at Chelsea. Honestly, being able to take my brothers and my dad to a box at Stamford Bridge is the most amazing thing in the world and a treasured memory for us all, and we've loved sharing that with them. We have so much gratitude for those experiences, but also for having you in our lives as a whole.

I also want to thank my extended family, all my cousins and friends who love me and who I love back. They know who they are, and there probably wouldn't be a page long enough to name every single one of them, but the love they've shown for me and how happy they are for me is incredible. They're not jealous, they just want me to go and do the best I can do, and I'm not sure they'll ever realise how much I appreciate that.

My other extended family is actually Anna's family, and I want to say a massive thank you to Conor, Jack, Helen and Gary. The way that they've helped me keep grounded and not lose my head, and the guidance they've given me about the ins and outs of the industry has been amazing. Conor and Jack feel like my brothers, and the way that Helen and Gary have brought me into the family and the household, as well as just allowing me to love their daughter as much as I do, is something I'll always be grateful for. A big, big thank you to them all.

Also, thank you to Anna's best friend, Brooke and her daughter Amelie. Amelie is the most beautiful, craziest kid ever, and I never thought I could love a child so much. I sometimes look around and think that I've just surrounded myself with the strongest people, but mainly strong women, and Brooke is one of them. She's the best parent and strongest mum, and I'm so happy to know her.

Special shout-out to all my mates, especially the gaming boys: Luke and Alfred the Great. They are the escape I never knew I needed. Each night, I can sit there and play *Call of Duty* with them and laugh and forget about what I've just done that day and not have to worry about the next day that's coming up. It's a big thing in my life. I love it and I love them.

But obviously, the mate I love the most is Harry Brown. He's been there for me since Year Seven in school and is an essential part of my life. Alex is the rock that I need at work, but Brown is the rock that I need in my life. If I've ever needed anything, if I'm crying about something or if I ever need help or advice, he's always been there for me, from the teenage years right through to today. If everyone in the world could be a little more like Harry Brown, it'd be a better place. He is amazing.

Also, big shout-out to the Brown family—Laura, Leanna, Vicky and Gordon—because they are literally my second family. I feel like I have a second mum, a second pair of sisters and a second dad (who tries to teach me how to play golf) in them. The golf never works, but the rest does, and they love me like one of their own, and I'll forever be grateful for that.

Now, onto my first and most important family.

Without all my brothers and sisters—George, Delilah, Alf (yep, you get two mentions) and Matilda—I would not be the person I am today. I wouldn't have that competitive edge if I didn't have my brothers, and I wouldn't have that funny side if I didn't want to make my sisters laugh. Everything I do in life, I do to make the people in my life proud, and they are a major part of my life, so I hope I continue to be as good a brother to them as they've been brothers and sisters to me.

I want to say thank you to my mum and dad for loving me and all of us kids so much. They have given me the best start in life, and I don't mean that in terms of money or anything like that, I mean through the pure love they've shown us, the happiness they've given us and the life that we grew up in, which they created for us. I love them both so, so much.

And, finally, Anna. You know how they say behind every strong man is a stronger woman? That has never been truer than with me and Anna. I will always be thankful to Anna for coming into my life, but also for continuing to be there. Not only was she the one who taught me how to love and fixed me from my past relationship, she's grown me as a character, and she's turned me into the man I always wanted to be. She allows me now to do this job, even though that's caused us so much heartache, and she's supported me the whole way. She deserves all the thanks and praise in the world, and I don't think any Acknowledgements page could quite capture how much I love her.

Thank you.